Industrial Ruins

Industrial Ruins

Spaces, Aesthetics and Materiality

Tim Edensor

Oxford • New York

First published in 2005 by
Berg
Editorial offices:
1st Floor, Angel Court, 81 St Clements Street, Oxford, OX4 1AW, UK
175 Fifth Avenue, New York, NY 10010, USA

Berg is the imprint of Oxford International Publishers Ltd.

Library of Congress Cataloguing-in-Publication Data
Edensor, Tim, 1957-
Industrial ruins : spaces, aesthetics and materiality / Tim Edensor.
p. cm.
Includes bibliographical references and index.
ISBN 1-84520-077-2 (pbk.) — ISBN 1-84520-076-4 (cloth)
1. Industrial archaeology. I. Title.
T37.E33 2005
711′.5524—dc22   2004028585

British Library Cataloguing-in-Publication Data
A catalogue record for this book is available from the British Library.

ISBN-13 978 184520 076 3 (Cloth)
ISBN-10 1 84520 076 4 (Cloth)

ISBN-13 978 184520 077 0 (Paper)
ISBN-10 1 84520 077 2 (Paper)

Typeset by Avocet Typeset, Chilton, Aylesbury, Bucks
Printed in the United Kingdom by Biddles Ltd, King's Lynn

www.bergpublishers.com

Contents

Acknowledgements

This book has been a labour of love, an exciting adventure into some of the dark and dank places of Britain. The numerous journeys have involved meeting and staying with friends and colleagues, as well as encounters with numerous hotel workers and the people who use ruins. The cost of these travels and the photographs that have been collected along the way have been supported by a generous grant from the British Academy. The efficiency of the excellent staff at Berg is similarly appreciated. In addition, as part of the process of thinking through some of the ideas in this book, I have presented material on ruins at a variety of conferences and seminars. I would like to thank Andrew Blaikie, Dydia de Lyser and Gillian Rose for inviting me to present papers, and particularly Karen Till for organising a very stimulating and enjoyable few days in Minneapolis, along with Alan Organschi, Thomas Lahusen and the staff and students who came along. In helping me produce a website and the photographs which illustrate it and this book, I am extremely grateful for the technical expertise and patience provided by Michael Cheung, Abid Qayum, Helen Brown, Albert Bowyer and Charlie. In addition, I give humble thanks to my colleagues at Staffordshire University, including David Bell, Tracey Potts, Maggie O'Neill, Gary Kelsall and Andrew Conroy who have supported me in my work, as well as the many graduate and postgraduate students who have had to listen to me blethering on about ruins. I have several exciting escapades and shared ideas with fellow ruin enthusiasts Caitlin Desilvey and David Papadopoulos, and I thank them for their great company and insights. Finally, as usual, all these travels would not have been possible without the forbearance and encouragement of Uma, Jay, Kim, Ji and Rosemary.

−1−

Introduction

As a young boy on long summer visits to my grandparents' cottage in Scotland, a particular ruin exerted a magnetic attraction for me. At the top of the steep, tree-lined country lane which led away from the cottage lay an area of extensive beech woodland. Nestling amidst the trees was a building known locally as the Haunted House, an imposing building designed in the Scottish baronial style that had lain derelict for years and was now the domain of owls, jackdaws and rabbits. It was crumbling and unstable, but I and my siblings ignored the barbed wire and the notices that warned of danger, and explored the remnants of parlour and dining hall that were now strewn with rubble. There was not much left of the building, few nooks and crannies or spaces that were not open to the sky, but at the back of the dwelling was a sumptuous wood with a collection of ornamental gateposts and a well; a wood that was the occasional venue for youths from the nearby village to carve their names on trees and drink cans of beer. The haunted house was part of a large estate that had been developed by a hugely wealthy rubber baron in the early years of the twentieth century. If you followed the road that skirted the wood, you came to the gatehouse, no modest lodge but itself a grand and exotic building which was the only inhabited part of the estate. Here lived an ancient woman who took it upon herself to maintain the estate to some degree and try to ensure that, as the signs warned, trespassers would indeed be prosecuted. With her dogs and a par-ticularly vicious goose, she patrolled the estate in an archaic automobile, whistle at the ready to summon help and frighten intruders, especially children.

The wood adjacent to the haunted house was our way into the estate, and more importantly, to the gigantic mansion that lay in the middle of the policies. The rubber baron had gone bankrupt as his estate neared completion, and whilst the haunted house and gatehouse had been completed, the big house had not been fin-ished inside and was bereft of plaster and furnishings, remaining thus for decades. It was this mansion that drew me towards it on most of those holiday days, despite the added fear of capture by the elderly crone or perhaps also partly because of that. A half-mile walk through the woods led to a steep decline through thick

woodland and undergrowth where the big house lay. The mogul had built extensive ornamental gardens surrounding the house which, together with the buildings and stone furniture, were designed to appear far older than was the case. A walled garden contained a fountain guarded on four sides by stone lions, and grass grew in its bowl, although if the spring was especially wet, frogspawn would collect in the murky water trapped there. The fountain was etched with rather morbid inscriptions: 'Yesterday returneth not'. Tomorrow perchance, cometh not'. 'Today is thine, misuse it not'. Occasionally, exotic blooms would force their way through the dense undergrowth and provide a splash of bright colour. At one corner of the walled garden was a favourite haunt, a gazebo, which acted as a hide from which deer, woodpeckers and other wildlife could often be seen, for the estate had become an unofficial nature reserve. From this point, a stone balustrade led to the woodland paths, paved but largely covered now with moss and a thick mulch of pine needles. The paths had been bordered with yew and pine hedges but in the decades following the laying of the garden, these had grown and formed an umbrella of dense foliage to create magical tunnels through the woods, which shut out much light and sound. In the woodland to the side of these tunnels, barely discernible through the undergrowth, were a few statues of strange lions and peculiar humanoid figures now covered in lichens.

Despite the freedom of movement available in the gardens, the house was thoroughly barricaded against intrusion unless one broke in through a window, and any smashed windows were quickly boarded up. One day, however, after many years contentedly exploring and playing in the gardens, I arrived at the house to find that a large window on the ground floor was wide open and it offered an opportunity to squeeze through to the never-inhabited house inside, an invitation that was, of course, impossible to resist. The gloomy rooms of the house, shrouded as it was by overgrown trees, gave up a number of extraordinary sights. The oddest was the display case inexplicably containing a stuffed, two-headed calf, perhaps a treasure from an age when freakishness and curiosities were desired. In a basement room, cinema seats from the early years of film were stacked in rows, together with slot machines and games which presumably had entertained the cinema-goers. And in an upstairs room with grand bay windows, littering the floor were the skeletons of hundreds of pigeons and song-birds who had found their way into the building through a small hole but had been unable to escape. After witnessing this macabre scene, and because the creaks of the building were heightened in the general silence, I didn't want to hang around as my imagination veered towards the uncanny and the horrifying. I left the house and went homewards to disclose my exciting adventure, and although I later regretted exploring only a small part of the mansion's interior, there was never another opportunity to gain access.

These powerful childhood experiences have remained in my memory since that time, but distressingly, for me, the ruined gardens and house have been transformed. For the property was converted into a country park but, following the failure of this venture, presently serves as a guarded, private estate where the mansion and surrounding buildings have been adapted into expensive flats. Accompanying these developments have been the renovation of the house and the transformation of the gardens so that they more closely resemble the original plans. The lawns are neatly manicured and the stonework of the fountains, walls, balustrades and gazebo has been cleansed of foliage and blasted clean of grime. Most strikingly, the tree tunnels in the woods have been disciplined into the shape of the hedged walkways they originally served as, replacing the unique with the commonplace.

As the above account indicates, I have been drawn towards derelict and abandoned buildings since my childhood. This is partly because of the local geographies I have been familiar with but was also stimulated, I think, because the promise of extraordinary sights and mysterious experiences is built into the popular culture of children with its myriad tales of adventures in secret gardens, magical labyrinths and dense, enchanted forests. For me, however mundane they may seem, ruins still contain this promise of the unexpected. Since the original uses of ruined buildings has passed, there are limitless possibilities for encounters with the weird, with inscrutable legends inscribed on notice boards and signs, and with peculiar things and curious spaces which allow wide scope for imaginative interpretation, unencumbered by the assumptions which weigh heavily on highly encoded, regulated space. Bereft of these codings of the normative – the arrangements of things in place, the performance of regulated actions, the display of goods lined up as commodities or for show – ruined space is ripe with transgressive and transcendent possibilities. Ruins offer spaces in which the interpretation and practice of the city becomes liberated from the everyday constraints which determine what should be done and where, and which encode the city with meanings. Accordingly, they offer opportunities for challenging and deconstructing the imprint of power on the city. For as Henri Lefebvre declares, for a progressive urban politics to be effective, 'the most important thing is to multiply the readings of the city' (1996: 159).

Ruins litter the industrial landscapes of the West although their prevalence varies enormously. For instance, in Britain, there are far more ruins to be found in northern and central England than in the more prosperous south. The production of spaces of ruination and dereliction are an inevitable result of capitalist development and the relentless search for profit. The quest for more profitable products, expanded markets and cheaper ways of manufacturing things, together with the inexorable quest for producing new goods and services, produces periodic crises of accumulation where surplus labour and capital drive down prices and profits. One response to such crises is to suddenly drop less profitable elements of the production process, often simultaneously moving production from one area or country to another, and then to devalue them so they can later be redeveloped. Those buildings disposed of in this fashion are thus temporarily or permanently rendered useless for industrial enterprise.

Ruins do not take one shape but are manifold in form, fashioned by the era in which they were constructed, their architectural style and their industrial function, and also partly depending upon the strategies mobilised by firms towards them after abandonment. Some are left to linger and decay for decades, turning into heaps of rubble over the years, whilst others stay for a while until the first signs of decay take hold and then are demolished, and some are eradicated shortly after abandonment. Often a ruined space is marked only by a vast expanse of concrete flooring, in which tiles, concrete and the traces of floor partitions are found. What might be at first a neat expanse of white, shimmering floor, is gradually taken over by plants, which seek out the cracks, burst through erupting concrete and gradually turn the flat surface to powder. The rate of decay also depends upon the constituent materials of the building and upon local industrial strategies. Authorities in cities that are able to attract inward investment are more likely to demolish derelict structures taking up space that might be used for new enterprises, whereas in cities which fail to attract new investment, there tends to be a greater prevalence of ruins. Abandoned buildings tend to be rapidly stripped of valuable assets and where this includes vital protective material such as doors, windows and tiles, the building is rendered less able to withstand the elements. Similarly, the intrusions of youth who enjoy smashing up windows, doors and walls erodes the ability of the building to remain insulated against the weather. The extent to which such damage is perpetrated depends upon accessibility to those who would pluck its saleable or useful contents and destroy its fixtures.

At present, there are not as many ruins as there were during the 1980s when landscapes of industrial ruination dominated whole areas of cities, as swathes of manufacturing suddenly became obsolete under economic restructuring. Several of the photographs in this book are from that era, the golden age of industrial ruination. At the end of the 1970s and through the 1980s, the right-wing Conservative government allowed 'market forces' greater rein than had been the case during the long era of 'consensus politics', in which governments of both major political parties adopted a somewhat protectionist response to the effects of industrial crisis. With the privatisation of nationalised industries and the scrapping of protectionist legislation, a pitiless restructuring of the economy rearranged the landscape of industrial

zones across Britain, as old, heavy industries sited in brick-built and stone-clad Victorian and Edwardian factories fell into disuse, the demolition of large chimneys being the most spectacular sign of this replacing of one industrial template by another. The economy geared up to welcome softer industries which required different kinds of industrial structures, such as airy offices, retail warehouses and single-storey buildings which could be left behind or dis-assembled according to strategic contingency. In contradistinction, these lighter, cheaper buildings, often more comfortable for workers and staff, produced more flexible entrepreneurial spaces than those characteristic of the more immovable edifices of brick and stone-built factories. Simultaneously, an orgy of real estate speculation took off which asset-stripped buildings occupied by 'uneconomic' enterprises or left them vacant, awaiting an economic upturn which would render such properties more valuable. Yet despite the large scale of industrial ruination through which industries and buildings were consigned to obsolescence, this was an uneven process. Many industries housed in old factories remained active, and some structures were effaced whilst others subsided into disuse, lingering on in the urban landscape but bypassed by other flows of money, people and energy.

Although they are currently fewer in number, a journey around the old industrial districts of most British cities continues to turn up derelict and abandoned buildings. These areas of the city, typically adjacent to railway lines and canals, amongst the huddle of buildings surrounding harbours, or amidst the scattered remnants of industry marooned within swathes of terraced housing and tenements, have often not been redeveloped to the point of total transformation. Indeed, the evolution of such areas has often been decidedly piecemeal and so they remain a part of the urban palimpsest featuring the industrial buildings of successive industrial eras, with the strong imprint of Victorian Britain still enduring. Although they are not as common as they were fifteen years ago, industrial ruins are still being produced out of the restructuring processes that were largely initiated under Thatcherism, and they are often structures of quite recent origin.

This book has evolved out of my enthusiasm for visiting industrial ruins, and spans three decades, primarily focusing upon the traditional manufacturing areas of north and central England and Central Scotland. The ruins I have explored and which feature here belong to Manchester, Stockport, Liverpool, Glossop, Stalybridge, Oldham, Blackburn, Burnley, Bolton, Birmingham, Stoke-on-Trent, Derby, Nottingham, Leicester, Grangemouth, Falkirk, Leith, Stranraer, Brynmawr, Luton, Southampton, Hull, Sheffield, Huddersfield, Newcastle, Sunderland and Hartlepool. This is the last time I shall refer to their location, for the arguments of the book would be less pertinent if they were accompanied by this superfluous geographical information, as I will shortly explain. As far as I was able to gather, I have toured ruins which used to be crushing mills, motor factories, garages, goods yards and depots, locomotive works, boatyards and chandlers, textile mills, tile factories and potbanks, chain manufacturers, foundries and steelworks, engineering workshops, rubber factories, dye producers and glass works, as well as numerous other indeterminate small workshops and warehouses.

One of the major objectives of this book is to contest the notion that ruins are spaces of waste, that contain nothing, or nothing of value, and that they are saturated with negativity as spaces of danger, delinquency, ugliness and disorder. I argue that such assignations point to wider social conventions through which space is endowed with meaning and function, something I have already discussed in terms of the political contexts which render spaces 'useless'. Such common sense depictions mask the social, political and economic processes through which decisions about space and value are reached.

In a conventional reading of the urban landscape, dereliction and ruin is a sign of waste and for local politicians and entrepreneurs, tends to provide stark evidence of an area's lack, that simultaneously signifies a vanished prosperity and by contrast, an uncertain future. According to such a conception, formerly productive spaces become rubbish, are no longer of any use, or have been used up. Clearly, the increasing rate at which ruins have been produced across the urban landscape of Britain is testament to the effects of faster modes of capital accumulation and the disembedding impacts of global capital flows, dynamic processes through which space is purchased, cleared and reassembled, deterritorialised and reterritorialised, producing practices which destroy urban space ever faster and more efficiently.

The dynamic colonisation of space by capital infers that all space has the potential to become lucrative, whether now or in the future. All space can be transformed from useless to prosperous and back again through investment and disinvestment. Ruins thus serve as a temporary rebuke to the notion that all space is abstract, the site of current or future production (Lefebvre, 1991), can be divided up, quantified and apportioned as property and exploited for profit. Accordingly, for those for whom space must have an evident function as productive or as property, such a purposive idea means that ruined space is understood as somewhere in which nothing happens and there is nothing. This kind of vision matches the concerns of property speculators. If spaces are conceived as disturbingly non-functional, they must be replaced and filled in – turned into abstract space – to remove these signs of unproductive and unfunctional blankness. Frequently, they are asset-stripped and then cleared to encourage property speculation because dereliction appears as a scar on the landscape composed of matter out of place, which must be erased and then filled in with something more 'useful'. Where local economies are depressed however, this may take the form of leaving ruined sites alone, until a time coincident with economic upturn when their redevelopment might be more advantageous. The ruins featured in this book are situated within this period of varying duration, between abandonment and potential future redevelopment. As Doron maintains, wasteland and spaces of ruination 'are created by suspension of new plans for an area' a suspension which is commonly represented on maps as a blank area (2000: 260–1), an impossible designation of space as *terra nullius*, which suggests they are spaces of and for nothing. However, such indeterminate inscriptions open up possibilities for their non-entrepreneurial use in the often lengthy period between abandonment and development or erasure.

The understanding of space as abstract which emerges out of dominant, capitalist modes through which it is appropriated and produced, is underscored by similar conceptions utilised by bureaucratic, governmental and planning operations, whose personnel usually come to similar conclusions about the nature of derelict space. For instance, the 'shell-ridden terrain' of former industrial sites, according to the Civic Trust, evokes 'a sense of lost vitality' (1988: 8). These negative impressions are compounded by perceptions about the uses which focus upon derelict space. It is a 'locus horribilus' (Grunenberg, 1997: 195) in which a range of deviant acts take place, activities carried out by people commonly identified as undesirable, and which promote fears of disorder and crime. But these assumptions about what ruined space is used for are not merely concerned with identifying cultural practices deemed to be 'anti-social' and thus consolidating ideas about the respectable uses of the city. They are also charged with aesthetic

evaluations: 'neglected land not only looks depressing. It also tends to attract fly tipping, graffiti and fly posting, all of which "uglify" the environment' (Civic Trust, 1988: 7).

The consignment of ruins to the common category of 'wasteland' necessarily obliterates the wide divergencies which exist between the characteristics of such spaces. According to such notions, wasteland is devoid of positive social, material, aesthetic qualities, or is purely an abstracted and quantitative entity technically identified by the assumed absence of activity or function. Yet ruins housed a wide range of distinctive industries, were and are sites upon which varied forms of dense sociality occur, possess rich histories, differ according to size, materiality

and their state of disrepair, vary with regard to the uses which are made of them by humans and other life forms and the ghosts which haunt them.

Thus in 2003, the latest report by CABE (the government-sponsored Commission for Architecture and the Built Environment), for instance, presents derelict land as a quantifiable entity that can be identified as inherently problematic (www.wastedspace.org.uk). The report declares that there are up to 70,000 acres of derelict land across Britain, including 5,000 hectares containing derelict buildings. With the ostensibly progressive intention of increasing the amount of parkland, playgrounds and other forms of public space available in communities, the celebrity-led campaign invites members of the public to nominate their grimmest piece of derelict land in Britain so that design-led initiatives and the 'efficient' management of space can reclaim and transform these areas. There is an explicit determination to minimise the effects of 'anti-social' activities in these 'blighted' areas, confirming that derelict land is identified with crime and 'deviancy', is again construed as ugly and is, moreover, indicative of a wider urban cultural malaise. It is particularly ironic that the multiple uses of ruins and derelict land as spaces of play are nowhere alluded to in the light of the avowed aim to build playgrounds since, as I will show, they serve as alternative play spaces for children and adults.

The negative notions of industrial ruination infer aesthetic judgements which widely diverge from the tradition of compiling celebratory accounts of non-industrial ruins. Highly aestheticised 'picturesque' representations derived from romantic perspectives have dominated writing on ruins, but rather than industrial ruins, these accounts have typically focused on classical or archaic ruins, crumbling medieval townships and castles, decrepit stately homes and the 'fake' ruins erected on eighteenth-century estates, and rural tumbledown cottages and farmsteads. These themes linger in contemporary depictions of these specific ruined forms so as to sustain an iconography of dereliction which largely bypasses contemporary urban ruins. Often the subject of poetic description and artistic endeavours, certain tropes resound through these representations, but these romantic themes are wholly unsuitable for accounting for the industrial ruins featured in this book.

According to the romantic aesthetic, the ideal ruin had to be 'well enough preserved (while retaining the proper amounts of picturesque irregularity) to produce the desired mix of emotions in the beholder' (Roth, 1997: 5). Thus the recently vacated building or the pile of debris do not qualify for such aesthetic appraisal. During the late eighteenth century, like many appreciations of 'nature', the representation of ruins in art conformed to specific aesthetic 'picturesque' conventions about which features should be foregrounded. Ideally, such representations should stress 'variety and contrast of forms, lively light and dark interplay, rough textures, and above all, rather busy foregrounds with assorted irregular trees or rambling shrubbery in one or both corners of the picture, between which a few figures and/or animals appear' (Hawes, 1988: 6). In paintings and engravings, this picturesque was also frequently conjoined by a conjuring up of the sublime, with stormy clouds and looming edifices depicting the requisite atmosphere of awe, or with an apprehension of the magical forces that remain unseen (see Jackson, 1988, for an in-depth discussion of these artistic tropes and Janowitz, 1990, for an exploration of ruin poetry).

These encodings emphasising the picturesque – and particularly the sublime – were allied to a sense of melancholia which saw ruins as emblematic of the cycle of life and death, symbolic of the inevitability of life passing, of a future in which obsolescence was certain and the inexorable processes of nature dispassionately took their toll of all things. And for humans, the natural world was that home to which our bodies and our buildings would ultimately return, despite any pretensions to immortality we might possess. Such a melancholic aesthetic tempered the optimism of modern industrial development, for ruins signified the transience of all earthly things despite the utopian promises of endless social advancement. The debris of the past – the ruined castles, abbeys, cottages and farmsteads – which littered the landscape of a newly industrialising Britain and was partly caused by rapid rural depopulation, displayed the brevity of existence and seemed to mock the claims of progress in the face of the inevitability of death and decay. Besides these local sites, as the classical ruins of ancient Greece and Rome became better known through the grand tour and the rise of classical scholarship, they revealed the seemingly inevitable demise of empires, a notion which pertinently quashed the hope that the spreading British Empire might establish perpetual rule over its dominions. Instead, these ruins seemed to prefigure imminent degeneration and

collapse. In a context in which vast sums were being made by industrialists, such concerns were tinged with a moralism which warned of the futility of amassing riches and power. A 'vain and obscure remembrance' was all that remained of the great 'classical' civilisations and the question was posed by Comte de Volney in 1791, '(W)ho... can assure me that their present desolation will not one day be the lot of our country' (cited in Hawes, 1988: 5).

The rise of industrialism and the rapid social change which it brought produced an intensified nostalgia for the past, and signs that revealed it became revered. Accordingly, ruins could be saturated with a host of imaginary romantic associations that testified to a bucolic past populated by charming characters. So profound was the cult of ruins that eighteenth-century wealthy estate owners created their own ruins as media for the remembrance 'of departed grandeur and of the transience and fragility of that which in appearance was indestructible; tangible warning to the living of the impermanence of stone and flesh' (Zucker, 1968: 198). In addition, these rural tumbledowns and archaic monuments served a nationalistic ideological purpose and they continue to be 'presented as iconic of British "heritage"' (Janowitz, 1990: 2). The visible remnants of the past which littered the British countryside could be reclaimed as 'the physical trace of historical event' which succoured the production of the imagined community of the nation. They seemed to materially testify to the ideological construction that Englishness/Britishness was immemorial, most specifically because they picturesquely blended in with the supposedly 'natural' rural realm as an expression of culture merging with the land (ibid.: 4–5). Yet again, underlying this celebration of the enduring lineage of Britain, doubts about the future of the nation crept in, since it simultaneously challenged 'the structure of the present, and threatens to eradicate eradicate temporal difference, swallowing up the present into an unforeseeable yet inevitable repetition of the past' (ibid.: 10).

Interestingly, Janowitz goes on to make an explicit comparison between these romantically apprehended ruins and contemporary sites of dereliction, contending that the 'twentieth century intention to ruinate has irrefragably changed that peculiar pleasure of ruin which comes from the contemplation of the absolute pastness of the past within the aesthetically controlled shape of temporal transience' (ibid: 1). This 'aesthetical control' through which such ruins are contextualised within an environment, so as to convey certain preferred sentiments and lessons is indeed not a feature of the industrial ruins discussed in this book. Neither is the contemplative impulse necessarily induced through wandering amidst contemporary ruins; rather there is an unpredictable immanence of impression and sensation. Yet intimations of transience are far from absent. Instead, the influences of the past emerge from a rather less controlled environment, one that is not devised to transmit ideological effects.

Rather than this romantic aesthetic, contemporary industrial ruins are more likely to epitomise a sort of modern gothic, part of a wider sentiment which emerges out of a 'post-industrial nostalgia' which focuses on 'dark urban nightscapes, abandoned parking lots, factories, warehouses and other remnants of post-industrial culture' (Grunenberg, 1997: 176). For a gothic sensibility, ruins possess the attraction of decay and death, and to enter them is to venture into darkness and the possibilities of confronting that which is repressed. These pleasures are of a vicarious engagement with fear and a confrontation with the unspeakable and one's own vulnerability and mortality, a diversion which is also a way of

confronting death and danger and imagining it in order to disarm it, to name and articulate it in order to deal with it. Representations of dereliction echo through resurgent popular gothic cultural forms which espouse the idea that the structures of the modern world are falling down, a notion which extends to an envisioning of the city as a disaster zone. Fuelled by millennial fears of apocalypse and the belief that a new medieval era is upon us, sentiments perhaps fuelled by folk memories and cruelties perpetrated in earlier eras, industrial ruins similarly question the persistent myth of progress. This impending decadence can be envisioned amidst a ruin where it is read as a macabre sign of what is to come, a symbolic space of darkness which prefigures future degeneration. As we will see, this topography of dismal decay courses through popular cultural forms, most notably in cinema where ruins frequently symbolise dystopian portrayals of a gloomy urban future.

While my reading of ruins is very different to these dark, pessimistic fantasies, gothic interpretations usefully foreground continuities with the romantic tradition in which ruins rebuke scenarios of endless progress, a notion that I will also explore, though as more of a critical appraisal which understands industrial ruins as symbols through which ideologically loaded versions of progress, embedded within cultures of consumption and industrial progress, can be critiqued. In addition, a gothic aesthetic 'revels in ruins, whether it be architectural, moral, biological, ontological or psychic' (McGrath, 1997: 154) in the sense that ruins epitomise transgression and the collapse of boundaries. For while it may veer towards the macabre and bleak, the gothic 'marks a peculiarly modern preoccupation with boundaries and their collapse' (Halberstam, in Toth, 1997: 89); it is concerned with the disintegration of the ordered. The gothic 'brings into shadow that which had been brightly lit, and brings into the light that which had been repressed' (McGrath, 1997: 156). Notions about disorder and hybridity are central to this book, although these are qualities which are celebrated for reasons at variance to the kind of dystopian pleasure which lovers of the gothic take in signs of decay.

While notions of a post-industrial gothic certainly captures some of the hybridities and transgressive spatialities of ruins, they can never escape connotations of gloominess and darkness, and tend to involve a wallowing in melancholia and sense of foreboding. It is my aim to acknowledge the blurrings of boundaries, and also the inevitability of death and decay. But I want to position this in a celebratory fashion, so that ruins are free from the gloomy constraints of a melancholic imagination, and can equally represent the fecund. They are sites in which the becomings of new forms, orderings and aesthetics can emerge rather than belonging to a 'sinister, crepuscular world' of death and stasis (Zucker, 1968: 195). While ruins always constitute an allegorical embodiment of a past, while they perform a physical remembering of that which has vanished, they also gesture towards the present and the future as temporal frames which can be read as both dystopian and utopian, and they help to conjure up critiques of present arrangements and potential futures.

This book is concerned with exploring the effects and uses of industrial ruins in a particular fashion. There are many alternative ways in which an account of ruins could be shaped. There could, for instance, have been a rigorous historical enquiry into the factories and warehouses visited, including details of production, industrial relations and perhaps a selection of oral histories from ex-workers and managers. Such an approach would no doubt have been interesting. However, I have not chosen such a course because I want to move away from specific forms of disciplinary knowledge and enquire about what ruins can tell us about wider social and cultural processes across urban space. In addition, I want to capture something of the sensual immanence of the experience of travelling through a ruin and my usual uncertainty about what went on within these abandoned buildings. The particular geographical locations of the ruins featured here are therefore not important to this endeavour, for assumptions about their embeddedness in imaginary geographies are likely to provide unwelcome interference with the more generic points I wish to make. That is why none of the photographs are labelled, for it is my wish that they evoke individual responses amongst readers without their being contextualised by surplus information. In addition, I hope that some of the photographs strike chords with the theoretical themes of the book – although not in any obviously illustrative fashion – but they may be utilised as an alternative source of information independent from the text.

Whilst some may point out that the themes of the book never foreground the visual as a means of apprehending and interpreting ruins, and there is therefore something of a contradiction in the provision of so many photographs, my response is to argue that photographs are never merely visual but in fact conjure up synaesthetic and kinaesthetic effects, for the visual provokes other sensory responses. The textures and tactilities, smells, atmospheres and sounds of ruined spaces, together with the signs and objects they accommodate, can be empathetically conjured up by visual material in the absence of any realistic way of conveying these sensations, other than through words and images. Photographs of ruins are also particularly valuable because whilst derelict sites are in a fluid state of material becoming, they can reveal the stages and temporalities of decay. As Roth observes 'by fixing ruins on photographic paper, we … have the illusion of reclaiming them from the further effects of nature and time – that is, from death' (1997: 17). Most photographs in this book along with many more can be found on my website (2002).

Two final points need to be made before I provide an outline of the organisation of this book. Firstly, in writing about ruins, it would be insensitive to ignore the

images of ruination which accompany war and it is indeed a sobering thought that the twentieth century has produced more ruins than ever before. As Roth asserts, twentieth-century wars 'have shaken our framing of ruins' (1997: 20). The most enduring recent image of ruination has, of course, been the remnants of New York's World Trade Centre following the attacks of September 11, 2001. I will not however, be discussing the ruins produced by warfare in this book, concentrating instead on the depredations wrought by cycles of capitalist reconstruction which either obliterate buildings or render their contents and the activities which they house instantaneously obsolete, turning solid things and places into air. Together with the effects of war, this vast scale of devastation reveals the 'enormity of our capacity for ruination' (ibid.).

Secondly, my travels around ruins are, to me, not particularly fraught with danger. One has to be aware of perilous structures and unsound flooring and rickety stairs, and numerous small scratches are incurred through trying to gain entry. However, I must acknowledge that for many, ruins would seem to be dangerous places, and the fear related to such concerns preclude many from entering them. Thus my gender and age are pertinent factors in making spectres of violence and predation absent from my imagination and from assumptions about what I might confront in derelict space. These factors have effectively rendered ruins accessible places for me to explore.

The organisation of the book is determined by its preoccupations. I am interested in re-evaluating industrial ruins in order to critique the negative connotations with which they are associated in official and common sense thought. Thus I am concerned to highlight the possibilities, effects and experiences which they can provide. Moreover, this reclaiming of industrial ruins from negative depiction is allied to a concern to show how they are exemplary spaces which can be used to critique ways in which urban space is produced and reproduced. Accordingly, Chapter 2 will examine the ways in which ruins are used to show that assumptions about their social uselessness, derived from assignations based on economic value and utilitarian notions of order, are groundless. I will detail the ways in which they are used as spaces for accommodation, ecological practice, adventure, play, recreation and creativity; look at how they circulate as symbolic spaces through popular cultural forms, especially cinema; and examine how they are used by non-human forms of life. Chapter 3 moves on to show how ruins, as particular spaces of disorder, can critique the highly regulated urban spaces which surround them. My argument is not that spatial order is unnecessary, but that the disciplinary, performative, aestheticised urban praxis demanded by commercial and bureaucratic regimes which are refashioning cities into realms of surveillance, consumption, and dwelling – characterised by an increase in single-purpose spaces – is becoming too dominant. These orderings are violated in the ruin which, once an exemplary space of regulation, has become deliciously

disordered. Ruins confound the normative spacings of things, practices and people. They open up possibilities for regulated urban bodies to escape their shackles in expressive pursuits and sensual experience, foreground alternative aesthetics about where and how things should be situated, and transgress boundaries between outside and inside, and between human and non-human spaces. Accordingly, ruins act as spaces which address the power embodied in ordering space. Chapter 4 specifically examines the ways in which ruins can assist us in questioning normative materialities. Continuing to explore the spacing of objects, I look at how ruins are emblematic of that which is assigned as waste, and the attendant assumptions about what kind of matter is surplus or integral to the city. I will discuss the effects of the material excess which is confronted in the ruin, and how the aesthetic and sensual charge of this excess can decentre the idea that objects are necessarily discrete, especially when they are assigned commodity status. Finally, Chapter 5 is expressly concerned with the spatialisation of memory in the contemporary city, maintaining that characteristically, memory is increasingly disembedded from its immediate social context though commodification and expertise, most notably through the production of heritage. The fixings that emerge from these processes are powerfully challenged by the sorts of memories that ruins offer. Ruins are already allegories of memory, but in addition, the involuntary memories which ruins provoke and the ways in which they are haunted by numerous ghosts foreground experiences of memory which are contingent, frequently inarticulate, sensual and immune from attempts to codify and record them.

More generally, this project is concerned with opening out the ways in which the city is used and interpreted. It mobilises a dynamic ontology in opposition to an ontology of fixed, immutable forms. The spatial aporias which surround us are neglected at a cost, fuelling monological readings of the city and restricting the diversity of practices and experiences, as well as constraining the ways in which forms of otherness are confronted. Concerned with a politics of urban becoming which appreciates the mysteries of the world, I want to highlight how the contingent, ineffable, unrepresentable, uncoded, sensual, heterogeneous possibilities of contemporary cities are particularly evident in their industrial ruins

–2–

The Contemporary Uses of Industrial Ruins

As the contemporary city becomes increasingly subject to regimes of regulation and demarcation, space tends to be divided up and assigned for specific kinds of activities, whether for shopping, playing, living or working. Challenges to these boundaries are policed so that, for instance, it is deemed inapposite to dance in shopping malls or to live or sell goods on the side of the street. Within this authoritative spatialisation, as I have argued, certain spaces are deemed suitable for nothing, are fenced off from those who would carry out activities within them, although it is understood that their functionless presence is only temporary, pending redevelopment. Industrial ruins belong to this assignation, and are, in official parlance, 'scars on the landscape' or 'wastelands' whose use-value has disappeared. Formerly hubs of dense activity within the city from and through which flows of people, matter and energy coursed from far and near, such ruins might appear quiescent and useless by comparison to their former state. Yet despite this redesignation of formerly industrial sites as spaces of waste, ruins are the site of numerous activities and very quickly become enmeshed within new social contexts, whether as part of the neighbourhood to which they belong or as sites that draw people from further afield. Ruins may become spaces for leisure, adventure, cultivation, acquisition, shelter and creativity. And as spaces that have been identified as waste, as well as 'dangerous' and 'unsightly', ruins also provide spaces where forms of alternative public life may occur, activities characterised by an active and improvisational creativity, a casting off of self-consciousness conditioned by the prying gaze of CCTV cameras and fellow citizens, and by the pursuit of illicit and frowned-upon practices. These uses contrast with the preferred forms of urban activity in over-designed and themed space: the consumption of commodities and staged events, a toned down, self-contained ambling, and a distracted gazing upon urban spectacle. Under-determined by the usually over-prescribed 'official' or 'appropriate' uses, the looseness of ruined space permits a wide range of practices. Doron (2000) shows how in a multitude of sites assigned the status of 'derelict' and 'void', or labelled 'dead zones' by architects and planners, space is produced in diverse yet unprescribed ways by 'transgressive' practitioners who hold 'raves', have sex, garden or dwell, expanding the possibilities and meanings of such realms. In this chapter, I will explore the varied uses of industrial ruins, focusing upon how they are sources of useful materials, temporarily occupied as a home, serve as spaces of adventure and play, and serve more mundane purposes. I will then go on to discuss how they are utilised by artists and film-makers and, finally, look at their use by non-human forms of life.

Before I look at the practices which surround these contemporary ruins, I want to consider briefly the use-value of such spaces by looking at a recent account of an iconic ruin of classical civilisation in Rome in order to identify the spatial characteristics which render ruins suitable for a particular range of activities, and also to look forward to the next chapter where I will discuss the ordering and dis-ordering of space. Christopher Woodward (2001) draws upon the compellingly rich and diverse evocations of Rome's famous Coliseum by writers and artists over many centuries, portrayals which highlighted the numerous uses to which the site was put. The Coliseum did not appear as it does today, but was a far more unkempt and unpoliced site. Travellers were drawn to the peculiarities and sur-prises which lay within the undisciplined, overgrown, underdetermined space it had become, a space in which people, animals and plants lived, and in which humans played and preached. As a result of these activities, the vibrant sensory space that was produced, together with the historical associations of the building, provoked a rich experience of fantasy and reverie. The Coliseum crumbled in this way for centuries, colonised by plants and plundered for building materials, but nevertheless was a significant attraction for these early travellers, partly because of this disarray. With the rise of Italian nationalism and a need to draw upon the glories of ancient Rome as part of the nation-building project, the antique site was reclaimed by the nascent Italian state in 1870 and interpreted according to the emerging rational, scientific norms of modern archaeological and historical cod-ifications. All extraneous material was expunged – plants, accoutrements, dwellings and other agglomerations that made it a place of life and evolution – and it became, according to Woodward, 'the most monumental bathos in Europe: a bald, dead and bare circle of stones ... (with) no shadows, no sands, no echoes', a highly regulated space that came to function solely as a tourist, historical mon-ument (2001: 30). Tellingly, he concludes that despite the welter of painting, prose and poetry that focused upon the Coliseum before this conversion, in 1870, he has been unable to find any comparable artistic works that have been inspired by the monument in the same way. The one exception he cites is Hitler, to whom it was a symbol and a monument of enduring power, testifying to the magnifi-cence of Rome, and thus could stimulate the Führer's own fantasy of achieving immortality through leaving a similar architectural legacy through the endeavours of the Third Reich. Woodward concludes, 'poets and painters like ruins, and dictators like monuments', and while this might be a somewhat hyperbolic statement, it eloquently identifies the ways in which use has become synonymous with organised function and the modern spatial ordering which sustains 'appropriate' practices.

Using Ruined Space

Plundering

Typically, shortly after they have been closed down and condemned as useless, derelict factories are asset-stripped so that most of the machines, furnishings and other surplus material identified as valuable are recycled through other industrial

plants or are sold. Such renderings usually do not affect the structure of the building, which remains insulated against rain and wind for a time, at least until entry is forced, windows broken and access thus becomes available for others. At this point, the denizens of the informal economy circle the building, checking out times when it is unsurveilled so they can engage in the silent work of plucking the tasty bits – any lead, stained glass, pieces of furniture, tiles, windows and doors and other treasures that lurk in basements, attics and boarded up rooms. Thus the ruin provides a temporary treasure trove for low-level entrepreneurs to exploit anything that can be recycled and sold on to junkyards, second-hand furniture stores and scrap metal yards.

This starts the process by which buildings get picked clean and start to disintegrate, contributing to the speed and process of decay. Simultaneously occurring with this illicit plunder, and taking place after it has been accomplished, other, less organised individuals enter the ruin and collect pieces of what remains, finding new uses for old bits of machinery, souvenirs that might be pinned to walls, artefacts and all sorts of found objects to decorate the home and garden. I have collected patents from the early years of the twentieth century, old posters instructing workers in the art of safety or pin-ups of mid-century celebrities and sporting heroes, cigarette cards, a winter jacket and cap from the Baltic states, rubber stamps embossed with illustrations of parts of machinery for sale, records of employment and letters of complaint from customers, and a brick bearing the label 'Utopia', as well as a host of bits and pieces of pleasing machine parts. In Stoke-on-Trent, I met a local man who had systematically plundered a large derelict pottery. First of all, he had gone looking into cellars and lofts and boarded-up cupboards and had discovered some prototypes of pottery designs, some of which were antique, with which he decorated his home and 'made a few bob'. Following this, he systematically appropriated fallen tiles, planks, bricks and sections of collapsed window frame in order to build a shed and a garage on his property. In addition, around autumn, many ruins are full of children collecting materials for bonfire night, often erecting large piles of timber on adjacent land (see Goin and Raymond, 2001, for American examples of similar uses of derelict industrial landscapes).

Home-making

In the 1980s, the processes of deindustrialisation coincided with the large increase in homelessness in Britain. The subsequent production of numerous ruins created places which could serve as temporary places of shelter and abode. The persistence of numbers of homeless people means that ruins continue to be utilised as a resource for temporary shelter, depending upon their state of dilapidation, by individuals and groups. Peremptory attempts are made to accommodate bodies in smaller spaces within the vastness of extensive shop floors. Planks and boards screen off spaces in which to sleep. Sheets of tarpaulin and bits of old sofas are arranged to create temporary homeliness, crates and boxes serve as tables or footstools, strips of cardboard become carpeting, and impromptu curtains are erected to curtail light and draughts. Nevertheless, given the likely short-term inhabitation, few attempts are made to provide decoration or an aesthetically modulated environment and accordingly, frequently surrounding those fixtures which accommodate sleeping or resting bodies is a ring of debris evincing that which has been consumed in this temporary home: newspapers, fast food takeaway containers, cigarette packets, empty drink bottles. A hunkering down in ruined space thus requires a different use of space to the normative modes of inhabitation in that here, space is marked out by debris and heterogeneous materials assembled to afford shelter and comfort, gathered around the body, together with clothing food and drink. Since this is a ruin, the necessity to keep things clean and orderly is not required, so fires may be lit on the floors for warmth and when a sleeping place gets too cluttered or messy, it is of little cost to move to a new site. Yet despite the contingent nature of this kind of dwelling, the need to mark and claim space is important and occasionally these inhabitants come over all proprietal, defending their residential space and reclaiming the notion of trespass for their own purposes. In most cases however, other users of ruins give these people a wide berth out of respect for their need for privacy and space. The unkempt and indeterminate space of the ruin, if it contains sufficient land bordering the factory, also means that it may offer the possibility for colonisation by gypsies.

Adventurous Play

Ruins are spaces of defamiliarisation which disorder the veneer of local appearances, rebuking the purposes to which the buildings were originally put. For many, ruins serve as an uncanny space amidst a familiar realm. But precisely because they are regarded as forbidden or dangerous spaces, they can become spaces of fantasy, places in which unspeakable and illicit acts occur, places of unhindered adventure. Ruins possess an allure for those who want to escape the increasing official surveillance in urban areas and the watchful gaze of neighbours and parents. For instance, they can serve as erotic realms where sex can take place beyond prying eyes, but by virtue of their proximity to settled urbanity, these endeavours may also be charged with the frisson of forbidden practice or fraught with the danger of being found out.

For children, industrial ruins contain the elements for all manner of playful activities, despite containing real dangers which anxious parents are likely to warn against. Many derelict factories are vast centres for exploration containing lengthy corridors to run along, stairs to scamper up, windows to climb through, trap doors, pulleys and channels to negotiate. Vast floor space and roofing are surfaces that enable the performance of spectacular and dangerous adventures, and numerous cupboards, cellars and offices provide confined felicitous spaces that serve as dens,

hidey-holes which may be fortified and furnished by the monstrous excess of debris. Feats of balance, agility and bravery may be accomplished in these extemporary playgrounds which, full of risk, clash with the insulated, smooth and regulated recreational spaces produced by official and commercial minds. Away from the regulatory instincts of parents and other adults, children may make their own rules and give full rein to their imagination, unchecked by the behavioural conventions imposed by their elders. So it is that the sheds and offices of ruins serve as dens for children's gangs, territories marked with signs of belonging – 'Keep Out' – and slogans of subcultural allegiance and tags. Car seats and sofas are organised into homely formations and rooms may be decorated with drawings and pictures from magazines. Objects from the outside world or found within the confines of the ruin contribute to the arbitrary placing of objects and the uncanny presence of things out of place. From the centre of the den, a place to chat, smoke and lounge, the ruin can be explored, a large unsurveilled space for play.

I was a victim of this unregulated activity in an enormous shell of a great rubber factory in South Wales, whose size engenders a sense of smallness and solitude in the visitor. Wandering across the vast shop floor during a particularly quiet part of the day, I became aware of a scurrying sound on the span of the spreading concrete roof, of footsteps and whisperings and stifled laughter. Every now and again, from above, a small cascade of particles descended from one of the large, ovoid, open skylights, falling close to me, followed by the audible patter of feet, but with no visible human trace. After some time, the attacks grew bolder. Rather than pebbles and twigs, the plummeting objects were large concrete chunks or bricks. The danger of the situation was apparent for with no-one else around, the gang of kids above, knowing their territory well, were able to subject me to unhindered assault, forcing me to retreat from the building.

Besides offering spaces for childish play, derelict spaces are also playgrounds for more adult pursuits, or those engaged in by both adults and children. Most evidently, ruins are places where people are able to drink alcohol and take drugs without being subject to surveillance. Used bags of glue, empty beer cans and bottles of spirits, roaches from cannabis joints, and the needles and silver paper of heroin users litter parts of many ruins. Whilst such spaces provide unguarded spaces for addicts to indulge their requirements, ruins also offer refuges for others wishing to hold disorganised parties and take illegal substances. In fact, derelict and empty industrial sites were ideal locations for the secret illegal raves that were held across Britain in the late 1980s to escape the constraints of zealous policing. Likewise, sex workers are able to use ruins as venues for their clients and under-age and other illicit forms of sexual adventure are enabled within the extensive spaces they provide.

These activities, frowned upon by respectable notions about what constitutes rational and suitable forms of recreation, are accompanied by another group of activities that may be regarded as tending towards the carnivalesque, those associated with destruction and vandalism. For spaces which are disordered, unkempt and unpoliced lend themselves to activities that may appear to be dystopian signs of an anti-authoritarian, to constitute a nihilistic rebuke to conventions of civil order and responsibility, but can alternatively be considered as entirely pleasurable adventures typified by a liminal letting go of the restraints which organise social life. The sheer pleasure in smashing things up is a sensation that can hardly be acknowledged in a highly materialistic culture, but this radical engagement with the material world, a desire to fracture and fragment, and to enjoy the delicious destruction of a variety of shaped matter is surely more than merely anti-social behaviour. In ruins, porcelain fitments are sent skittering across the floor to shatter upon contact with walls, boxes and sinks are hurled onto concrete so that they will spectacularly splinter, fragments bouncing across the floor. Larger structures, brick walls and plaster ceilings can provoke a challenge to the amateur demolition worker who must work out what techniques and forces must be assembled to produce their destruction, whereas lighter partitions of plasterboard can be ripped asunder with gratifying ease. Overturning stable objects, tumbling things downstairs or dropping them down lift shafts, spilling out lubricants or piercing water tanks so that liquids course down the storeys of a building; all are pleasurable activities which are usually forbidden but allow a spectacular engagement with the materiality of the world. There are rarely any windows in a ruin which remain intact and this testifies to the universal enjoyment of shattering glass by throwing projectiles, the gratification of the shattering sound and the pleasing spraying out of the formerly whole material. And this is also the case with the urinals and toilets where attack with bricks or metal objects leads to an easy fracturing. Alternatively, the specific targeting of placed objects or windows can be considered as games of skill. There is then, a pleasure in this kind of destruction, a visceral, sensuous demolition of space and fixtures that will likely be subject to the wrecking ball in any case. The satisfaction gained through creating explosions of noise and dismembering a variety of objects in different ways take place in a context where orderly maintenance and preservation are irrelevant. There is sensual pleasure in watching the slimy oozings of tipped over industrial substances, in seeing how plastic coagulates and bubbles when set alight, in making *ad hoc* piles of materials to knock over and in smearing messages and designs across crumbling walls with industrial residues. The joy reaped from being able to act out of control can be an irresistible inducement to corporeally engage with matter in this way, especially since such stuff is usually protected by surveillance and convention. The materiality and status of the ruin as waste mean that it is constituted to accommodate these spectacular deviant acts.

I watched a group of teenage boys doggedly trying to puncture a large cylindrical vat containing thick oil. Using a variety of implements, they finally found out that by erecting an assembly of planks, they were able to send very heavy objects rolling down at the tank so as to weaken its increasingly indented surface. The final stages of the operation required attack by a series of metal poles and as the sides of the container finally split, a continuous gush of oil flowed down to a hollow in the ground nearby where it formed a black pool, the mid-afternoon sun reflected in its still and even surface as the thick flow oozed out, draining the receptacle. This pool itself acquired purity in its sleek, perfect surface, and quickly became the new focus of attention, as the boys hurled objects into it, causing slow ripples and small splashes. The oily mere was filled with plastic toys, sacks, boulders, pipes and other debris, and came to resemble a tar pit in which the preserved forms of extinct life lingered.

These frowned-upon practices are complemented by other lawless pursuits. Ruins are ideal places to empty the contents of stolen handbags and safes. More evidently, they are sites to which stolen cars and motorbikes can be taken. At once, the goods yards and factory floors provide an environment where cars can be driven and the layout of obstacles can serve as improvised circuits for adventurous forms of joyriding. Wooden doors can be driven through in emulation of spectacular actions from television and cinema, adjacent objects can be collided with and sent flying, and vehicles can be skidded, turned over, set alight and detonated.

These affordances that make driving in ruined space so pleasurable – long stretches of concrete flooring or tarmac, wooden stairs, chutes, kerbs and other props and obstacles – also make ruins a rich playground for skating, skate-boarding, motorcycle scrambling and mountain biking as will be discussed later. Outside the prohibited public realms and the organised half-pipes and skateparks, the ruin offers a range of obstacles and surfaces which can be negotiated at speed. Besides the insides of the derelict factory, the gardens outside, replete with rubble and mounds, provide challenging contours to surmount and race around, a practice ground for the development of skills. Climbers too, use the walls of the ruin to build up competencies for further ventures. These more evident pursuits are also complemented by the rather less purposive forms of exploration that take place by urban inhabitants who are drawn to the marginal spaces in their locale, a form of non-spectacular tourism that roams across uncultivated commons and a range of urban areas that are supposedly unattractive (for instance, see Halgreen, 2004). On a more organised scale are groups of urban explorers who, attracted to active as well as derelict buildings, are drawn towards ventilation shafts, disused tunnels, towers, drains, sewers, bridges, underground complexes, mines, disused quarries, churches, prisons, military sites, old hospitals and asylums. According to the accounts compiled by participants, the motivations for such explorations vary from those attracted to architecture and history, the sensual dimensions of such places, the subversive, anti-authoritarian nature of such pursuits, the adventure-some physicality of such endeavours, and the thrill of the risk entailed. In the case

of the latter motivation, urban exploration is akin to the expansion of adventure sports which seek out thrills and 'peak' experiences at variance to an over-regulated and usually quiescent life. Informed by an ethics which takes a dim view of vandalism and the right to transgress regulatory regimes, and equipped with torches, hardhats, climbing equipment, face masks and goggles they enter these often forbidden zones, usually at night, frequently with the aim of exploring the least accessible parts of the complex. Taking photographs and writing accounts that record their adventures, these groups communicate and encourage their practices through invisible networks of association, typically via the numerous websites dedicated to the subject (for instance, see http:/www.geocities.com/urbexers; http:/www.infiltration.org; http:/www.urbex.org.uk).

So the ruin is marked as a site where a host of playful, adventurous activities are carried out. By virtue of the affordances of derelict factories and the loose ways in which they are regulated, they present opportunities for carrying out leisure practices which would be frowned upon in more regulated urban space, activities characteristically based around physical expressiveness, the transgression of normative relations between people, space and things, and around affective collective endeavours that tend towards the carnivalesque. Like other demarcations of spatial activity, these are generally consigned to private and marginal spaces (Shields, 1991), but they reinscribe the carnivalesque in an increasingly smoothed-over urban environment.

Mundane Leisure Practices/Ruins as Exemplary Sites
Despite the attractions of ruins for a range of carnivalesque and playful pursuits, it would be neglectful to ignore the numerous mundane uses of ruined space by people as part of their everyday practice, habitual and unspectacular activities which sew space into routines and perhaps are part of what might be identified as 'practical' leisure, pursuits conventionally regarded as 'rational' recreation and which contrast with the activities identified in the above section. Again, ruins provide unpoliced, extra space where such everyday pastimes are carried out. Most obviously, ruins are simply spaces which are incorporated into the walks of urbanites, supplementing the myriad tracks which flow across the city. Despite the fact that it is an officially reviled space, the ruin continues to be woven together with the rest of the city through these pathmaking exercises, whether as part of contingent travels or as part of a regular route along which to walk a dog. Wasteland also provides space for people to tether grazing ponies and erect jumps for horses. The shortage of land in the city mean that tracts of overgrown flower beds or landscaped lawns can now serve as alternative allotments for gardeners, who may grow vegetables and fruit; and ruined land is often used to cultivate marijuana plants which, fostered on land which seemingly belongs to nobody, makes criminality difficult to identify. As I will shortly discuss, wasteland and rubble are quickly colonised by

flora and fauna and thus attract birdwatchers and botanists. In addition, ruins serve as extemporary, free car parks and as places to dump rubbish since they cannot be 'spoilt' more than they already are. These creative uses of local space are part of the mundane and habitual practices through which people engage with ruined sites, opportunistically utilising that which seems to be temporarily underused, and entwining that space into regular quotidian or weekly rituals, in which situated practice becomes unremarkable, perhaps unreflexively performed.

This creative, rational use of derelict space for leisure practices, along with the more carnivalesque forms of play discussed above, highlights the dearth of communal areas in many urban realms as space becomes divided up into functional spaces, turned into private property and surveilled to guard against inappropriate pursuits, diminishing the availability of common land. These appropriations show that ruined buildings and land can act as exemplary spaces in which alternative urban practices can be performed. And more conscious, political projects can utilise wasted space. In 1996, thirteen acres of derelict land on the site of a demolished Guinness distillery in Wandsworth, London, were occupied by some 500 protestors in a bid to provide a prototypical, exemplary eco-centric urban community as a means to protest about dominant forms of land use, the pre-eminence of property ownership, planning priorities and urban development and thus more generally to imagine urban life and culture otherwise. The occupation lasted for five months until the protestors were evicted and the whole site bulldozed. Wittily given the name 'Pure Genius' after a Guinness advert, the site was described by the occupants as 'Wandsworth Eco-Village' and 'London's first permaculture visitors' centre'. In addition to using the site to experiment in carrying out small-scale, environmentally sensitive agricultural practices, the community aimed to show that derelict sites could be used for co-operatively run, sustainable and low cost urban housing, a model that was counterposed to the profit-seeking extension of high-cost private housing in rural areas.

A motley collection of dwellings and other buildings – yurts, domes, pyramids, tepees, benders and adapted vehicles, greenhouses, a community 'roundhouse' – were assembled on the site, constructed from a range of scrap materials. Similarly, gardens were rapidly developed and planted to serve as a food supply and as a location for creative horticultural design. The site became a venue for a host of social and cultural activities and the learning of skills, including story-telling, circus stunts, the creation of murals, painting and sculpture, drama and music. Equally important was the party ethic which informed the production of the site as a space for expressive cultural practices through which identity was expressed, a carnivalesque realm in which affective engagement and the pursuit of pleasure was given full rein (Halfacree, 1999). Accordingly, the project was able to advertise how 'enterprise', 'creativity' and 'self-help' could be charged with alternative meanings to those inscribed in consumer and business culture. Moreover, these

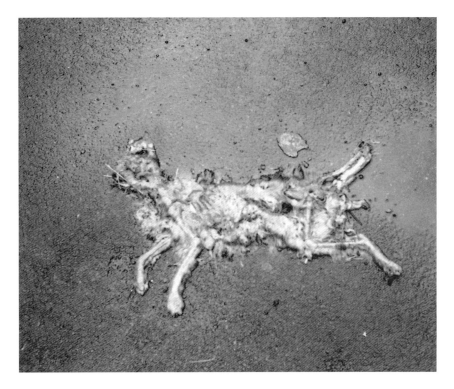

aims were furthered by co-operation and collaboration between various 'tribes' (Maffesoli, 1996) possessing disparate political beliefs to produce experimental modes of social organisation. And in addition to drawing all these different groups together, attempts were made to reach out and involve local people in the project so that the site could be brought into local politics and relationships.

Pure Genius served to provide an innovative way of exploring the possibilities of direct action by achieving a distance from normative urban space, where a collective could 'begin to expand its own agenda rather than being fixed within the imaginative structure provided by the opposition' (Featherstone, 2003). Moreover, because of this distance, the project could 'suggest ways in which in which the broad green movement can engage with urban politics linking environmental and social justice issues' (ibid.). An autonomous space was created and temporarily controlled by a heterodox selection of 'alternative' groups, and this facilitated the forging of networks and associations between them, and the production of a symbolic challenge to hegemonic ways of ordering the world. Because of the great media attention that the Wandsworth experiment attracted, there was considerable success in broadcasting the aims and achievements of the project, so that it became educative and exemplary. Yet despite this moderate success, as it became widely known, the openness of the site meant that it became a magnet for the homeless, alcoholics and drug addicts, some of whom rendered the environment potentially violent and crime-ridden, and sapped the energy of participants who were not familiar with the skills required to absorb such people into the transient community. Such a dilemma can be seen to result from the dearth of public spaces available for experimentation and alternative practices and forms of sociality.

The above discussion has served to show that ruins are potential sites for a range of social activities which differ from those usually accorded preferential status in the city, for they are not regarded as 'respectable' and 'appropriate' in the inscription of urban norms of conduct. Moreover, such activities contrast with those practices which sustained forms of sociality and social relations grounded in the previous spatial order at these sites, namely those organised around industrial production. Instead of being directed by compulsion and the internalisation of rules of comportment, practice and social engagement, the relations with space described above are forged through affective and enthusiastic desires rather than through the compulsions of urban and industrial order. Furthermore, social bonds may be locally constituted and consolidated by the coming together of adolescent gangs and homeless citizens, by dog walkers and gardeners, or they may be formed through more extensive networks, for instance by loose collectives of 'urban explorers'. All these practices constitute alternative communal uses for urban space which stitch ruins back into localities, broaching their mooted separation from smoothed-over space.

Art Space

Ruins are unpoliced spaces in which a host of artistic endeavours may take place, blurring the distinctions between practices deemed transgressive and rational. Most obviously, they provide a extensive area of vertical surfaces for the inscriptions of graffiti artists, for graffiti is an almost ubiquitous presence in those ruins in which access is easy. Especially when these are concentrated on the internal walls of the derelict building where they cannot be seen by neighbouring residents, there is little sanction against graffiti, since it makes little difference to a site already identified as unsightly and excessive. In these favoured sites, graffiti ranges from the wall-to-ceiling coverage of all planes in a riot of colour, turning buildings immersed in the grey and brown hues of dereliction to spaces adorned with multi-coloured effusions of names and cartoons, to the crude daubing of football and music slogans and gang names; and from the humdrum inscriptions of obscure tags and monikers to the detailed, complex works of graffiti 'artists'. Occasionally, the embellishments of extensive multi-coloured illustrations blend with the fractured roofs, large puddles and intrusive plants to create scenes extremely rich in texture and hue. Ruins thus provide unsurveilled urban spaces for graffiti artists to develop their alternative aesthetics and skills, for where graffiti has been largely regarded as 'out of place' in the more regulated spaces of the city (Cresswell, 1996), its presence is more ambivalent in spaces of dereliction.

In addition to graffiti, ruins are used for all sorts of impromptu artistic endeavours. In the next chapter, I will discuss the profusion of unusual juxtapositions contained by ruins, where things usually kept apart mingle and stand on top or next to each other. Whilst these assortments may be arbitrary, it appears as if certain arrangements must have been fabricated and carefully organised. The opportunity to play with objects and other forms of matter unselfconsciously is afforded by the lack of any surveillance and other onlookers and by the range of material that is often to hand. Accordingly, improvisatory sculptures suggest that they have been wrought by visitors at play. It is not surprising that such works are made, since twentieth-century artists have loosened ideas about the constituents of art works, making liberal use of waste materials. Drawn to its varied textures and forms, and its symbolic qualities, the aesthetics of rubbish are familiar through the work of such artists as Robert Rauschenberg, Kurt Schwitters, Joseph Beuys, Tony Cragg and David Mach who have used waste in rich, divesre ways (Hauser, 2002). These enthusiasms extend to art made by members of the sustainable art movement, which champions the ethical use of industrial by-products and debris into art. Such artistic usages of waste matter create 'an alternative economy' and encourage observers to question processes of '(de)valuation and exclusion' (Assman, 2002: 72).

Sometimes ruined industrial spaces are utilised as part of larger schemes of artistic display. One recent exhibition, Radioactive, organised by the Sozo Collective as part of a bigger project entitled Re:location, took over a substantial ruin in Smethwick, Birmingham, which had previously been an x-ray factory and earlier had been a workshop for an automobile manufacturer (http://www.re-location.org.uk). After spending three months partially renovating the building, turning rooms into exhibition spaces and living quarters, and simultaneously producing art works for display, the collective organised the two-week exhibition. This ambitious and experimental event attempted to recontextualise and give renewed purpose to the building through a number of creative strategies reflected in the art. Works tried to convey the physicalities and social relations embedded in the working conditions of previous workers, they utilised found materials to forge sculptures and pictures, and they created works that dramatically clashed with the ruined industrial space: a Japanese garden in a corner of a large goods yard incorporated the already growing plants that had colonised the buildings. In addition, a large collection of photographic plates found *in situ* were curated as part of the exhibition, vestiges of graffiti and posters left by workers were retained and highlighted, and the site simply served as a different kind of gallery space for hanging painting and installations. The multiplicities of the ruin were creatively explored by these artists to collectively produce a multi-faceted exhibition which explicitly drew upon the materialities, spatialities and histories of a site to provide a dramatic contrast to conventional kinds of display and the venues in which they occur.

In a different vein, one fascinating use of an abandoned industrial landscape is Emscher Park in the northern Ruhr, Germany, where a collection of architects, artists, gardeners, scientists and planners have created what they term an 'imaginative landscape out of industrial dereliction' (Latz and Latz, 2001: 73), on the site of a vast iron and coal complex. Out of the coke plants, blast furnaces, ore bunkers and manganese depots, they have created a heterogeneous landscape. Some areas have been allowed to decay and others have been re-presented as giant sculptural forms. The collective decree of the producers is that rather than possessing instrumental values which inhere in industrial spaces, 'fantasy should allow us to use the abstraction of the existing structures in new ways, and so adapt the present system of organization to the appearance of chaos' (ibid.: 74). In addition to these aesthetic innovations, recreational uses have been created, so that large edifices have been turned into climbing walls, huge bunkers and a gasometer have become venues for diving, and other spaces have been designated as a location for parties, an adventure playground, and the display of art and exhibitions. Accessibility has been enabled by the construction of walkways which criss-cross the whole structure. By allowing the reclamation of ruined space by plants and animals to simply occur in certain areas, by decontaminating blighted spots, and through the deliberate fabrication of ponds, meadows and spectacular gardens, the designers have created a hybrid melange in which some places have been creatively transformed whilst others have been left alone.

Representing Ruin

In the romantic era, painting and poetry were the preferred media of representation for enthusiasts of classical and medieval ruination. In present times, a different cast of explorers and artists are attracted to industrial ruins. Despite the notion that they are useless and undesirable spaces, and despite their apparent marginalisation, ruins find their way back into economies of popular representation, circulating through television programmes, films, advertisements and pop videos. Besides my own website, several photographers have established engaging websites furnished with images of industrial decay (see the list of websites in references). Most evidently, commercial film makers are particularly drawn to ruined factories and warehouses as appropriate settings for a predictable range of dramatised events. The representation of industrial ruins in films exposes, and is imbricated within, certain cultural assumptions about the negative qualities of contemporary cities and urban processes, particularly proffering dystopian visions of a bleak future. Yet simultaneously these derelict realms may be conceived as a refuge from the relentless corruption and surveillance of these unhappy worlds. I will now outline four tropes through which ruins are represented in contemporary cinema.

First of all, industrial ruins provide a suitable backdrop for spectacular action. The costs of enacting explosions and extravagant forms of destruction need not generally concern film-makers, since the ruin has already been marked as wasteland and damage to property is thus inconsequential. Moreover, ruins possess a host of fixtures around which action sequences may be choreographed, gunfire may resound and physical fights can be played out across various vertical and horizontal levels. Various characters do battle in these scenes of ruination, consolidating the symbolic associations of ruins with forms of deviance and danger. They provide lairs for criminals and deviant gangs who commit illegal acts within these refuges and are often subsequently hunted down and confronted in these same

spaces. They also act as ersatz sites for military conflict, connoting the destruction wreaked in war. In a recent cinematic version of Shakespeare's *Richard the Third* (1995), the final shoot-out scene was filmed around the burnt-out shell of a 1920s power station in London. And in the Vietnam war film, *Full Metal Jacket* (1985), Becton, an abandoned 1930s gasworks adjacent to the River Thames was used as the Vietnamese city of Hue, since director Stanley Kubrick thought that the 1930s functionalist architecture of the gasworks was similar to that city's buildings. Further detailed ruination of the site to simulate war damage was carried out but the suitability of the pre-existent three-dimensional rubble and what Kubrick referred to as 'those twisted bits of reinforcement' saved the producers millions of pounds. Abandoned buildings similarly feature as sites where criminals hide and police pursue them in television serials such as *The Bill*. But they may also be identified as safe spaces in which the persecuted may hide.

Enemy of the State (1998) tells the story of an ordinary but successful lawyer who is unwittingly drawn into attempts to reveal the complicity of senior political figures with a scandalous political crime. The scene is created for the production of a climate of fear and paranoia, created through the hyper-surveillance of a government intelligence agency out of control and with the usual rogue elements. Super-efficient spy satellites, which are able to locate and identify their human

quarries from space, are able to penetrate most urban space via visual technology and listening devices. The renegade scientist, Brill, offers to help the protagonist in his attempt to escape the misplaced charges against him and bring corrupt politicians and the agency to book. Crucially, the susceptibility of most urban environs to penetration by surveillance technologies is contrasted with Brill's hideout, a ruined warehouse and undetectable home which he calls 'the Jar'. Outside the normal pathways of city life, the Jar is an ideal place for the patriotic but maverick scientific genius to hide in. The building was actually the rather iconic original Dr. Pepper plant in Baltimore, a concrete building in an industrial area of town surrounded by warehouses and truck stops, and it was demolished as part of the plot.

Secondly, often also containing extended action sequences, many contemporary science fiction movies feature ruins to signify an imaginary future of decadence and dystopia, which signify social breakdown or the aftermath of a global war, a landscape containing the remnants of civilisation evocative of the gloomy gothic aesthetic referred to in the previous chapter. Such venues are host to a range of denizens including Dr Whos, replicants, stalkers, demolition men, outlaws, visionaries, techno-geniuses, cyber-punks and spectacular gangs. One of the best examples of this sort of film is *Robocop* (1987), which depicts a future crime-ridden Detroit, where huge corporations have taken over most social functions and are driven by a desire to maximise profit at all costs. Like many other recent science fiction and horror films tinged with this contemporary aesthetic, the film is 'driven by both despair over the disintegration of traditional production processes and post-industrial nostalgia for the recent past with its illusory promise of stable and homogeneous social structure' (Grunenberg, 1997: 196). Omni Consumer-Products (OCP) controls the distribution of products, and even the embattled police force. Murphy, a distinguished and dedicated police officer is killed in the line of duty, but OCP integrates his brain and a few remaining features with state-of-the-art technology to form Robocop, designed to revolutionise law enforcement. In the course of his battles with criminal gangs, Murphy rediscovers his humanity as he unearths corporate corruption and abuses of power, and he endeavours to bring justice to Detroit outside the remit of programmed goals. The scene in which Murphy is killed prior to his rebirth as a cyborg, as well as the climactic shoot-out, were filmed in the abandoned steel mills of Monessau, Pennsylvania. Utilising the setting as a spectacular stage upon which violent action can proceed, the derelict ruin metaphorically accentuates the breakdown of an imperilled society but, as with *Enemy of the State*, it is also a refuge from the corporate world of surveillance.

Thirdly, we can identify those films which sometimes nostalgically lament the passing of the industrial landscape and way of life, particularly in British northern cities. Realist accounts such as *Brassed Off* (1996), about the struggles faced by former workers and their families in such typically depressed, post-industrial settings, feature the now deserted factories as symbols of former vitality in contrast to the quiescent present. In *The Full Monty* (1997), the abandoned iron forges and smelters of Sheffield are used to echo the uselessness of male labour habituated to a working life in a steel industry which has drastically trimmed its workforce or relocated. Following a kitsch and relentlessly optimistic promotional film about 1970s Sheffield which champions the steel industry that underpins the city's present and future prosperity, the first 'present-day' scene ironically depicts the unemployed protagonists unsuccessfully attempting to smuggle out a steel girder from one such empty factory in the now depressed locale. Within this wasteland topography of the declining steel town, inscribed by the casual wanderings, enforced leisure pursuits and schemes of the unemployed men to 'get by', ruins provide resources for the characters. As large, uninhabited stages, they serve as safe venues in which the men can practice their stripping routines without fear of ridicule or sanction, and thus help them to restore some dignity to their quest for meaningful labour, adapt to changing gender roles, and make a few quid in the process.

Finally, ruins also serve as sites which – by virtue of their place on the margin – are locations for more celebrated subjects and their activities, identities and practices which are conventionally regarded as 'deviant' but are positively reclaimed. Through such representations, ruins may be aestheticised, even eroti-cised. *My Own Private Idaho* (1991) features derelict property reclaimed by a sub-culture and used to accommodate an alternative, gay lifestyle; and Derek Jarman's *Jubilee* (1977) likewise shows carnivalesque sex and violence in a decaying England. These themes perhaps reach their apogee in Jarman's impressionistic *The Last of England* (1987), in which England is portrayed as a blighted urban waste-land. In the context of the radical industrial restructuring presided over by the Thatcher government, the derelict spaces and ruined industrial complexes of East London metaphorically conjure up social devastation and decay. And whilst this

backdrop conjures up a bleak vision of England characterised by excessive greed, terrorism, and homophobic and racial violence, these ruined scenes are also the site for alternative cultural identities and practices, the home of squatters and punk rock tribes, and are eroticised as sites for transgressive homosexual acts. These kinds of depictions also resonate with a contemporary gothic aesthetic.

Such gothic resonances are also prevalent in particular kinds of popular music, most obviously in that which is characterised as 'Goth' and in disparate kinds of post-punk 'industrial' music (for instance, in the work of Pere Ubu, Bauhaus, Nine Inch Nails, Throbbing Gristle, Einstürzende Neubauten and Test Department). In terms of lyrical imagery, album cover art and the very sounds created, such music conjures 'the post-industrial disappearance of the labouring body against the back-drop of vacant factory yards, deserted farms, bleak downtowns, a polluted envi-ronment and ever-present TV screens', a dismal topography within which 'boundaries between the "normal" and the pathologized "other" collapse' (Toth, 1997: 89–8). 'Emanating from the ruins of the urban-industrial space of the West' (ibid.: 88), together with gothic forms of film and literature and comic illustration, such sounds evoke a geography of despair, of 'growing up in manufacturing ghost towns' (ibid.). For instance, according to Hannaham, 'many Joy Division songs sound as if they were recorded in the deserted school buildings, abandoned factories and under the lonely buildings of Manchester' (1997: 94). Alternatively, the uses of industrial tools such as acetylene torches and electric saws as instruments which created sound through being applied to scrap metal and other waste materials were utilised to reimagine the now absent 'labouring body juxtaposed with the haunted ruins of industry' (Toth: 1997: 86).

In romantic times, artistic forms based on rural and classical ruins were typically represented by painters and poets. The imagery and aesthetics of the contemporary industrial ruin are mainly exploited through the cinema and in some of the marginal realms of popular music, although ruins are also used by contemporary painters, photographers and sculptors, and in some contemporary writing (for instance, in the work of Bertholt Bluel, 1998 and W.G. Sebald, 2002). Thus although ruins are frequently vilified spaces, they are not as neglected as these negative assignations might suggest, for derelict spaces continue to circulate through popular representations and other artistic forms. Whilst I have shown that there are a limited range of themes through which ruins serve as metaphoric backdrops for cinematic stories, their physical qualities can be transmitted through the screen, and their textures, atmospheres and aesthetics can potentially undermine their incidental positioning as spectacular, visually apprehended stage sets.

Nature Reserves

Besides the numerous social and representative practices through which ruins are utilised, they are also sites which teem with non-human forms of life, highlighting what Simmel refers to as the 'vitality of opposing tendencies' in that they are simulaneously 'sinking from life' and 'settings of life' (1965). As Roth proclaims 'as things fall apart, out of their remains emerge new forms of growth' (1997: 2). As spaces that have become unpoliced and are no longer regularly cleansed to minimise non-human intrusions, plants and animals show their adaptability to the opportunities which arise in the city as they quickly seek out cracks in which they may prosper, finding nesting spaces, food sources and territories. This rapid colonisation testifies to the scale of ongoing human attempts to banish from urban settings all but the most favoured companion plants and animals from their midst. And it also showcases the agency of insects, birds, mammals, fungi, shrubs, flowering plants and trees (Cloke and Jones, 2002) in the constitution of the urban, despite their wrongly assumed absence.

As far as plants are concerned, the rate and the nature of their colonisation of derelict space is contingent upon specific regional ecologies. The nature of growth depends upon factors such as soil acidity or alkalinity, on whether land is contaminated by metal or ash, on whether the factory was brick-built or fashioned out of particular kinds of stone, on the nature of rubble and on the surrounding geology. Plant ecology also depends upon which particular plants move in to take advantage of their favoured chemical and climatic conditions, for such plant-scapes are also determined by chance. Nevertheless, several species have particularly adapted to urban environments and are suited to move into ruined spaces, namely those fast-growing plants with intricate root systems which produce large numbers of seeds able to germinate quickly. So it is that a familiar sight of derelict space is of the silken seeds of the rosebay willow herb breeze-borne, parachuting through the wasteland and beyond where the seeds will land and send out runners into any surrounding soil. Other, equally ubiquitous plants include buddleia which becomes especially noticeable when it attracts crowds of butterflies and bees in summer. A hotch-potch of green blankets the outer grounds of ruins, gradually creeping into spaces where light and space permit growth, progressively blurring the distinctions between inside and outside. Fat Hen, dock, nettles, brambles, sorrel, horsetail, ferns, groundsel, chickweed, thistles, knotweed, ivy, the dense blanket of convolvulus leaves interspersed with its white trumpet flowers, and plantain and other grasses create this often dense mat of green, composed of varied shades, textures and shapes of leaves and stem. Rising above the undergrowth appear taller forms of vegetation: elder, willow and silver birch trees, hawthorn bushes and the much-feared giant hogweed. The mantle of green is complemented by splashes of different colours: the purples, blues and pinks of the intrusive Himalayan balsam, forget-me-not, foxglove and willow herb, the crimson of poppies, the strong yellows of ragwort, dandelion, celandine, coltsfoot, buttercup, evening primrose and stray rape plants, the gleaming white of michaelmas daisy and cow parsley, as well as multi-coloured lupins. Inside the ruin and on its outer walls, mosses, lichens and liverworts start to cloak the building and shaggy caps, puffballs and less edible fungi nestling amongst undergrowth or on rotting wood also colonise the outside and interiors. These verdant scenes are supplemented by escapees from nearby domestic gardens and the remnants of ornamental shrubs and rose bushes which bordered the buildings of factories and were designed to pleased the eye of visitors and the office workers in adjacent offices.

The botanical colonisation of derelict land and buildings is not a static process but changes over time depending upon the longevity of the abandoned site. Gilbert (1989) has identified successive stages in which particular plants predominate. First of all, grasses and quickly colonising plants move in (what he calls the 'Oxford ragwort stage'), and these initial colonisers prepare the ground for larger and taller perennial plants (the 'tall-herb stage'), and if the land is left for several years, these in turn give way to grass (the 'grassland stage'). Finally, the ecology becomes more stable and typically becomes home to trees and shrubs (the 'scrub woodland stage'). These phases of plant colonisation also influence the kinds of animals that live there. For instance, grass cover encourages the presence of large numbers of voles and mice, thus attracting their predators, whereas shrubs and trees provide shelter for nesting birds. This evolution of particular successive plant

ecologies introduces distinct forms of temporality into ruined space. Formerly a realm regulated to retain fixity, to ensure reproduction of the same order, ruined industrial space is now subject to ecological temporalities – at least until redevelopment of the site occurs – far removed from the temporal routines which used to characterise factory production. One might say that factories, which were devoted to the transformation of nature in the form of 'raw materials' into manufactured goods, when ruined return to nature once more, and are subject to its temporalities as the illusion of permanence dissolves.

Ruined spaces are equally hospitable to animals. It is evident that insect life is abundantly provided for with the decay of matter. Woodlice burrow into expanses of rotting wood, spiders weave their webs across ceilings and corners unhindered by dusters and vacuum cleaners, and ants lay claim to any neglected surface. Birds also quickly colonise ruins. Highly adaptable scavengers who are unfussy about where

they live and what they eat, pigeons take advantage of the openings presented by shattered windows to build nests in attics and roost along shelves and beams, ledges akin to the cliffs they frequent elsewhere. Other large birds such as magpies and jackdaws, already present throughout cities, take advantage of the chance to dwell in derelict space and the vegetation which surrounds it, as do wrens, blackbirds, starlings and sparrows, kestrels, gulls, house martins and swallows. Certain birds prefer rubble, such as the black redstart, a rare migrant to Britain, which proliferated after it made its home amongst the post-war bombsites of London. When redevelopment covered over these vacant sites, the redstart moved home to the weird surroundings of nuclear power stations, where a similar wasteland environment could be found within their perimeters. Other animals lay claim to ruins as well. Mice and rats abound. Foxes quickly colonise adjacent areas of land dense with undergrowth and lose their fear of entering buildings, hedgehogs move in and bats hang in ruined lofts until they swarm out into the evening air.

A prevalent desire for a controlled urban nature leads many of the plants found in ruins to be labelled 'weeds', 'the botanical equivalent of dirt … plants out of place' (Cresswell, 1997a: 335), assignations that metaphorically chime with conventional conceptions of ruins as blots on the landscape and ridicule the prevailing botanic order imposed by landscapers and gardeners. Often considered exotic and desirable blooms in Victorian times, certain plants which inhabit ruins, such as hogweed, rhododendron, Japanese knotweed and Himalayan balsam are now viewed as pestilential and tough adversaries in the battle against excessive vegetation, and have been recoded as weeds. Such views are consolidated by the ways in which some plants make human progress through ruined space difficult, announcing that they have taken over use of space. Nettles and thistles sting, robin round-the-hedge and brambles snag and pull at trouser bottoms and roots and tendrils trip up bodies if they move too fast. These troublesome weeds are symptoms of an unruly nature in the same way as animal 'pests', who become evident presences as they move out of their ruined refuge through more cultivated domestic and public urban space, transgressing their assigned marginal or rural

locations. The feared threat posed by these beasts reveals that nature penetrates urban existence, and foreshadows what might happen if is not controlled.

The succour provided by ruins to animals and plants and the ever-ready tendency of species to move out from their confines violates the rural-urban dichotomy. Unlike the tamed and pruned nature that is found in parks, gardens, landscaped areas and is embodied by domesticated animals, wild species do not respect normative patterns of urban order established to keep wildness at bay. And as far as animals are concerned, it is their retention of a 'constitutive wildness', genetically and physically unshaped by deliberate human fashioning (Palmer, 2003b: 51), that is connoted by their encroachment on purified space, as they move outward to steal food from dustbins and create litter, spread disease, prey on domestic animals, eat plants in gardens, shit on pavements and drives, and frighten urban inhabitants. Plants also invade and seed manicured areas as spores float across the city, colonising prized flower beds. The return of the agency of the wild, the role of plants and animals in producing space, becomes evident, transgressing the assignation of nature and underlining the threat posed by the ruin, for as Whatmore and Hinchcliffe declare, '(t)he fecund world of creatures and plants as active agents in the making of environments remains firmly outside the city limits, and those feral spaces in the city that most sustain them are cast as "wastelands" ripe for development' (2003: 42).

Yet these versions of a bounded urban space ignore the ways in which the urban is always a 'complex articulation of multiple networks connecting cities to other sites and trajectories through the comings and goings of materials, organisms and elements as well as people' (ibid: 44; also see Massey, 1993). For within the city there are a host of other sites which accommodate forms of wildlife, such as cemeteries, gardens and allotments, railway sidings and road verges, back gardens, parks, golf courses and river banks. Ironically this may be because as plants and animals seek refuge from an intensively policed countryside and forms of agricultural production which flood terrain with pesticides and herbicides to eradicate their presence, the less regulated areas of the city become refuges for forms of life displaced from the rural. Animals and plants in the city are thus always enmeshed within a network of relationships that extend into the 'rural', that space which is conceived as the opposite of the 'urban' and usually considered to be the realm of the 'natural', the place *for* non-domesticated animals. These biotic flows between the urban and the rural through which life-forms endlessly move foregrounds the presence of wildlife corridors criss-crossing the city, the largely invisible tracks along which animals mark territory and forge hunting and scavenging routes, and plants extend roots and seeds, often utilising channels which have been fabricated by humans, such as sewers and railway lines.

Needless to say, as they become 'swallowed up by the urban', animals must adapt their lives 'to deal with increased human control over, and presence in' the places

they inhabit (Palmer, 2003a: 66). They must negotiate hazards ranging from 'traffic, domesticated animals, lack of food supply, pollution, increasingly intensified urban-isation' (ibid.) and the presence of other creatures who have also adapted to the urban, whether feral animals or those which have developed symbiotic relationships with people. Thus, for instance, derelict land may provide good cover in which rodents may prosper, in turn affording ideal hunting territory for kestrels and other birds of prey, but this food supply is also likely to serve the activities of domesti-cated cats. Just as humans impinge upon non-human environments, animals and plants are rarely in any sense purely organisms belonging to the non-human realm of the 'wild' but are continually shaped by the constitution of historical, social (including both non-human and human socialities) and geographical processes.

I have argued that the intrusions of plants and animals into spatial contexts where they are 'out of place', through which creatures exercise 'unbidden, impro-vised, and sometimes disruptive energies in the ordering of urban space' (Whatmore and Hinchcliffe, 2003: 43), threatens the conventional orderings of rural and urban. The city is considered suitable for domestic pets but not for live-stock and feral animals, and only for certain wild species. Zoning delimits the presence of plants and animals, consigning them to specific places on the edge of cities or in wildlife 'reserves' within the urban or rural, yet in derelict space, such zoning policies are rebuked by the multifarious forms of life which prosper in spite of decisions that consign them to be out of place. Yet the desire to see certain forms of wildlife – although not others – in cities highlights the numerous moral ambi-guities and contradictions that surround the place of animals and plants and

challenge us to think about how cities might become a 'zoopolis – a place of habitation for both people and animals' (Wolch, 2002: 734). For instance, Griffiths, Poulter and Sibley (2000) reveal the ambivalence felt towards feral cats in Hull. For some, their inhabitation of derelict sites is conceived as disorderly, but for others, it feeds desires that look for and celebrate signs of nature, and in the case of these feral cats, they are conceived as wilder and closer to their 'true' nature than their domesticated cousins. The same might be said of the pleasures many urbanites gain from sighting foxes in their streets and gardens, and from coming across the vibrant colours of poppies, willow herb and Himalayan balsam along with other plants attracted to derelict sites.

More strikingly, because they are no longer subject to the application of weed-killers, pesticides and fertilisers, as well as rural methods of extermination, insects and slugs, nesting birds, rodents and foxes find a home in the increasingly thick undergrowth of ruined space, and thus the ecological value of such sites within the urban can be high. An apparently blighted landscape in Canvey Island in Essex, hemmed in by a superstore and a derelict oil terminal, an 'oasis in a landscape of oil refineries, new housing, massive roundabouts and drive-through McDonald's' (Vidal, 2003), a terrain replete with industrial and household debris, might be described as wasteland. However, it has been described as 'England's little rain-forest' because of the density of its rare wildlife population, notably of insects and moths. Created by the debris dredged up as silt and laid down over the land, lacking the features valued as 'beautiful' by conventional aesthetic adjudications of the rural, and subsequently used by children who have burnt grass and cycled and thereby restricted overwhelming tree colonisation, this post-industrial land-scape does not at first sight seem to conform to notions of what is ecologically valuable. In the same fashion, assignations of ruined and derelict land – which host large populations of beasts and plants – as wasteland, and as 'useless', are highly partial for they neglect the uses made of such sites by non-humans and their role in diversifying urban ecology.

This interpenetration of the urban and the rural, or of the social and the 'natural' reveal the arbitrary divisions that create such binaries and their spatial mappings. The ways in which animals and plants, as well as humans, produce urban space, most conspicuously at sites such as ruins, call for what Whatmore and Hinchcliffe describe as a 'recombinant ecology', a concept which acknowledges the dynamic reconfiguration of urban ecologies through the ongoing relationships between people, animals and plants (2003: 39). Since the impact of erasing large numbers of ruins at once would be considerable in terms of diminishing the richness of urban ecology, it seems particularly inapt to identify ruins as dead spaces, con-ceived, in true colonial fashion, as *terra nullius*, devoid of value, purpose and life. For like all forms of urban and rural space, ruins are heterogeneously co-produced by humans and non-humans (Murdoch, 2003) which are connected to the site by numerous flows, routes and networks of association. Nature is thus not in any sense pure and distinct from the humans but part of the hybrid environments to which both belong, which they both create, and which constrain and enable their activities.

Conclusion

This chapter has been concerned to show that far from vacant, waste spaces in which 'nothing happens', industrial ruins are thickly woven into local leisure prac-tices ranging from the carnivalesque to the mundane, and have been utilised as exemplary, experimental spaces from which to broadcast possible alternative eco-centric, artistic and social futures in the city. Representations of industrial ruins are woven into popular culture, typically serving as stage sets for cinematic portrayals of dystopian futures, spectacular action, dissident identities and nostalgia for the demise of socialities based around heavy industries; all forms of depiction which testify to popular conjectures about the characteristics of the contemporary city and its future. Finally, in expanding ideas about sociality to include the non-human use of ruins, we can identify the ways in which many derelict sites serve as excellent urban nature reserves, helping to confound the binaries between urban-human and rural-'natural'. All these practical uses are at variance to conventional notions about what urban space ought to be used for, and they are enabled by lack of surveillance and regulation, by the under-determined characteristics of ruined space. There are few surveillant cameras and little of the disciplinary gaze of others, few preferred routes along which bodies are channelled, and little semblance of material and spatial order to suggest that bodies should engage with space in preferred ways. In addition, the impact of the unruly affordances of ruins on bodies, and the subsequent coercion of people into entanglements and performances which disrupt normative understandings about what to do, promote scope for reflexive improvisation. Accordingly, the practices identified above hint at the disorderly effects of ruins, and their performance further contributes to assumptions about this perceived disorder. In focusing more tightly on the characteristics of ruined space, the next chapter explores these notions of urban order and disorder in greater critical depth.

–3–

Ruins and the Dis-ordering of Space

In this chapter, I explore the kinds of space ruins produce and discuss how they rebuke contemporary notions about order and its constitutive 'goodness'. This will serve as a celebration of ruinous spaces which unfolds into a critique of contemporary processes of ordering urban space. I am particularly concerned with challenging prevailing forms of spatial organisation, specifically via the production of order through distributing objects, functions and people, through the enforcement and habitual repetition of performative habits in particular places, and through the aesthetic encoding which produces normative visual conventions across space. As dis-ordered and messy sites, ruins provide a contrast to the increasingly smooth, highly regulated spaces of the city. Occurring in the back roads and interstices of the urban fabric, ruins deride ideals which champion the virtues of seamlessness.

Spatial Ordering and Disordering

Modernity seems to have been riven by two opposing forces, namely the quest for a seamless order and the simultaneous desire to transcend a regulated life, to enter into a realm of surprise, contingency and misrule. Scientific processes classify and fix meaning, and there is a yearning to banish ambiguity from what we might call a logo-centric modernity, but the desire for order is also a response to memories of earlier chaos and to the unsettling, dynamic nature of modernity where everything that is solid turns into air. Rojek (1995) distinguishes this will to order the world, the 'Apollonian' tendency, from the 'Dionysian' urge within modernity, which seeks out the antithesis of this regulation in the carnival and the unbounded, in excess and obscenity, in the sensual delights that flow through flux and the mixing of people, activities and desires. Lash (1999) identifies this romantic resistance to modern classifying and regulatory tendencies in an 'aesthetic reflexivity' which revels and accepts indeterminacy. The tension between these two modes of modernity is described by Berman as emerging out of a dialectical process whereby 'one mode of modernism both energises and exhausts itself trying to annihilate another' (1982: 165). The simultaneous production of order and disorder and the tension between them – often expressed as an ongoing attempt to vanquish each other – is highly uneven, especially within a context in which the speeding up of social change produces a variegated range of responses to the evaporation of previous certainties. Nevertheless, it is my argument here that as far as these tensions are currently worked out in the Western city, they are increasingly typified by attempts to regulate space, things and people so that Apollonian manifestations of modernity are uppermost. Thus the contemporary production of urban space is coterminous with regulation, surveillance, aesthetic monitoring and the prevalence of regimes which determine where and how things, activities and people should be placed. A machinic apparatus of policing, planning regulations, zoning policies, place-promotion, preferred forms of capital investment, the bounding of discrete spaces, the regulation of flows of traffic, people and money, together with flexible systems of information gathering permits a continual regulatory adjustment to conditions, as part of a 'modulated' society (Amin and Thrift, 2002: 45).

Processes of spatialisation are enmeshed with these modern regulatory instincts, and have emerged out of several interrelated processes. The designs and schemes of modernist planners to rationalise the landscape are embodied in the structure and organisation of industrial and domestic techniques for spatial control which form part of the 'machinic episteme' (Lash, 1999), the belief that an all-encompassing design can order meaning through the logical placing of people and things within a grid-like system. The grid delineates the functions of specific areas so as to produce a series of single-purpose spaces where preferred activities occur, creating what Berman terms 'a spatially and socially segmented world – people here, traffic there; work here, homes there; rich here; poor there' (1982: 168). Such spaces are internally regulated to exclude extraneous matter and subjects, partly through the instantiation of common-sense conventions about arranging social practices and placing objects. The designation of ruins and derelict land as particular kinds of negative spaces serves to illustrate this consignment of multiple features and functions into singular designations. This is also revealed in the wilful spatial divisions erected between the 'natural' or rural and the urban, despite the extent to which the city is continually broached by animal and plant agency, as discussed in the previous chapter.

Sibley terms this process the 'purification of space' to suggest 'a distaste for or hostility towards the mixing of unlike categories, an urge to keep things apart' (1988: 409). Strongly classified or 'purified' spaces thus 'maintain conformity' through their clear boundedness and the prevalence of centralised regulation. They contrast with 'weakly classified spaces' which possess blurred boundaries, are associated with 'liberation and diversity' and in which activities, objects and people mingle, allowing a wide range of encounters and greater self-governance

and expressiveness (ibid.: 414). Processes of ordering lead to the demarcation of zones, routes and areas for specific activities, producing connected single-purpose spaces and a geography of centres, terminals and unidirectional flows. The bounded forms typical of such a regime of spatial production might be characterised as commodified, hidden, inaccessible, 'prickly', uncomfortable to occupy and subject to intense surveillance (Flusty, 1997).

Processes of delineating space also assign subjectivities to space, creating social orderings 'which foster conformity and constrain deviation from very particular classed, gendered and racialised behavioural regimes, in which work and leisure, domestic and civic life, all have their proper place' (Whatmore and Hinchcliffe, 203: 41). Thus the delineation of a purified space implicitly identifies the 'outsider', the stranger or the 'other', as 'out of place' (Cresswell, 1996). Such subjects are surveilled, monitored and controlled and may be allocated to marginal spaces typically represented as dangerous, chaotic and dirty, the antithesis of 'purified' space (Shields, 1991). Paradoxically, such places on the margin are also imagined as realms of desire, permitting of interconnection, hybridity and possibility by virtue of their 'weak framing', synonymous with the tropes of colonial desire which centred upon spaces of perceived 'otherness' designated by colonial regimes of spatialisation (Kabbani, 1996).

Most obviously, the maintenance of orderly spatial assignations and prohibitions is carried out by the overt monitoring enacted by security personnel in spaces such as gated communities, and through the widening use of surveillance techniques, most notably CCTV cameras across central urban areas. This 'soft control' (Ritzer and Liska, 1997: 106) means that all people are potentially under surveillance at any time, but also provides the technological means to exclude 'undesirable elements' and activities. Thus, rather than the 'motion and turbulence that makes the city so appealing' (Squires, 1994: 83), unrestricted movement is discouraged in many of the new urban spaces. Congregating in groups is conceived as a threat to public order or as 'causing an obstruction'. Injunctions against 'squeegee merchants' who offer to wash car windscreens as they wait at traffic lights for money prohibits the work strategies of those seeking employment, and rules against sleeping or resting on benches and floors impose restrictions upon the movements and strategies of the homeless. Samira Kawash shows how simultaneously representational and material 'technologies of exclusion' produce a 'legitimate' public who have rights to their space as opposed to homeless 'usurpers'. The denial of any place through which homeless bodies may dwell or pass through generates a condition of 'perpetual movement' borne of placelessness, movement undertaken by the homeless not 'because they are going somewhere, but because they have nowhere to go' (1998: 322–9). Notions of order also include the values of circulation (of money, activity, people and things), of continuous flow, with the attendant fear of stagnant, slow and decaying places (see Highmore, 2002). More broadly, activities which confound these flows, such as 'loitering', 'hanging out' and lounging on the pavement might be deterred, considered potentially criminal, and particular activities such as 'cottaging' and 'begging' are particularly scrutinised. Sanctions range from the advice to 'move on' by security guards and police to more draconian stop-and-search police procedures when pedestrians are adjudged to be suspiciously 'out of place'. The channelling and containment of human flows across the city, then, reproduces a sense of what space is *for*. The internalisation of these spatial norms about how to act in urban space also fosters a reflexive monitoring of the self and a watchfulness towards fellow urbanites, self-surveillance and the surveillance of others.

For a planned spatial order informed by the requirements of industrial discipline, 'rational' recreation and consumption is also devised to socialise citizens, to be conducive to the formation of 'good habits' and 'appropriate' behaviour. Thus notions about self-control in public space, about what comprise appropriate postures, ways of moving, dress and voice modulation pervade pedestrian action. Transgression of these norms can earn direct confrontation with agents of order or the more subtle rebukes offered by the scornful glances of passers-by. Either way, regimes of urban behaviour are consolidated and act to suppress the body's expressivity and the range of sensations experienced. Such instructive regimes implicitly champion specific forms of sensual experience, producing a reflexive body which has become 'the training ground for the double process of educating the senses and making good use of them' (Frykman, 1994: 67) within an ordered space that fosters a rationalised, uncluttered sensory experience. In this case, the designs of planners are echoed in the impulses of some modernist architecture to remove all clutter so that the senses of modern urban subjects might be rationalised, for instance, in the belief that clear, linear sightlines allow purposive progress and an undistracted mind.

These normative, regulatory modes of perception have percolated into popular social conventions and cultural tastes associated with notions about what is 'civilised', and further, into reflexive self-development, so that the acquisition of sensory capabilities – taking the seaside air, cultivating a nose for perfume, developing a finely tuned ear for music and a taste for good food – are complemented by the bureaucratic monitoring of noise and smell. The de-odorisation of urban space, the restrictions of sounds and the encoding of a visual order render contemporary cities devoid of rich sensual as well as social experience. Consequently, a public space in which difference and disruption was sensually confronted has become restricted, and sensory deprivation suffuses the contemporary Western city as regulated tactilities, sounds, aromas and sights become predictable and unstimulating (Sennett, 1994). The production of tactile sterility can produce few niches in which various creatures might dwell, hide or loiter and cajoles bodies to act in accordance with the preferred performative norms. As I will argue, this production of seamlessness is simultaneously part of the manufacture of highly coded and themed aesthetic environments which order the gaze of urban dwellers.

These processes appear coterminous with contemporary projects to reinvent and re-brand cities following the demise of manufacturing industries with which they were once associated. Rather than focusing on attracting manufacturing plants, Western city strategists are increasingly likely to appeal to a mix of service industries, potential middle-class inhabitants, shoppers and tourists, policies which engender a particular approach to producing city space. Primarily, spaces of consumption multiply and are managed to facilitate consumer-oriented activity as opposed to other practices. Often typified by the 'serial monotony' of corporate outlets (Harvey, 1989) and homogeneous, semi-private shopping malls, the less regulated, more heterogeneous market-places of old are replaced or turned into themed spaces. As Debord states, 'social space is invaded by a continuous superimposition of geological layers of commodities' (1987: 41–2). Others have pointed to the diminution of public space and the subsequent growth of private spaces and the production of themed areas, in which designers have 'learned from Disney' in the combination of social control and aesthetic recreation.

This is particularly pertinent with regard to the emergence of festival market-places, heritage areas and cultural quarters which are themed to simulate historic

'atmospheres' or mediatised worlds (Gottdiener, 1997; Zukin, 1995; Sorkin, 1992) and where intensive theming, visual encoding and material order provide an illusion of seamlessness. The pervasive production of a normative semiotics of place deters the facility to decode space in ways at variance to preferred meanings, tending to thwart an enjoyment of the inevitable inconsistencies that prevail in all spaces. This aesthetic encoding reinforces notions about how urban culture is presented and staged, where things should be placed, and how difference should be contained. For instance, the 'exotic' and the 'different' are situated within a spatial ordering where the charge of otherness provided may be separately highlighted; but its isolation from the cluttered complexity of other artefacts, humans and images which constituted its original material and social context tames its alterity and fosters the construction of a landscape of display and spectacle.

It seems that in recent years, the desire to paper over the city – to fill in the blanks, to erase the jagged remains of shells that were once filled buildings – is more manic. The fabric of the past must be trampled down or converted into a sandblasted approximation of its former self, functioning as private accommodation or office space. In this smoothed-over landscape, interstices, fissures, cracks and margins within the urban fabric are more difficult to identify – as road systems, landscaping, an influx of retail warehouses, and new businesses fabricated out of glass, steel and plastic cladding, heritage spaces and shopping districts fill up the city. And the notion that the city must put forward a seamless, smoothed-over appearance to signify prosperity, to attract tourists, new middle-class inhabitants, investors and shoppers is not only articulated by planners, bureaucrats and entrepreneurs but embedded in a wider consciousness where it shapes articulations of the public good. For instance, the Civic Trust report (1988: 8) cited in Chapter One claims that a 'single gap site in a street can look as unfortunate as a missing tooth', implying that the city's smile urgently needs an appropriate filling if it is to seduce would-be investors. Moreover, although we have seen that ruins are widely used informally by urbanites and others, the same report avers that their presence imbalances 'the intricate social and economic patterns of the neighbourhood ... (and can) dissipate the sense of townscape' (ibid.: 6), dragging areas down. Aesthetic judgements, moreover, reaffirm this out-of-placeness, so that ruins and areas of dereliction exist outside the 'visual and social order of the rest of the community' (ibid.: 8).

Despite this frenetic impulse to smooth and encode, the longing for less regulated spaces continues to shape urban space. Popular desires for the contingent, fragmentary and ever-changing aspects of the carnival are co-opted by advertising and marketing strategists, who produce spaces to promise a cornucopia but offer a 'controlled diversity' rather than a realm of 'unconstrained social differences' (Mitchell, 1995: 119). Such spaces are familiar enough by virtue of their design codes, spatial organisation and thematic emblems which emerge from films, pop music and advertising. For example, the heritage landscape, with carefully devised street furniture, information boards, and reconstituted cobbles follows the imperatives of theatrical design. Producing a nostalgic simulacra of urban living, refashioned areas conjure up the signs of urban vitality or the atmosphere of a festival. But instead of the carnivalesque, this imagery and ambience tends to produce 'sites of ordered disorder' (Featherstone, 1991: 82), satisfying what Chris Rojek calls 'the timid freedom of respectable leisure' (1995: 80). The impact upon the moving body of this spatial containment and commodification has been the encouragement of a 'controlled de-control of the emotions' (Featherstone, 1991: 78), which includes toned-down, self-regulated forms of physical expression in which a sensual frisson may be experienced rather than an enveloping of the senses and emotions, in accordance with 'appropriate' ways of performing in the city.

Notwithstanding this commodified containment, rougher, more ambiguous places continue to exist, although they are usually consigned to specific times and marginal spaces (Shields, 1991). There remains a lingering fascination with the possibilities available at weakly regulated occasions and spaces, a desire for the sensual, disorderly experience of raves (Thornton, 1995; Saunders, 1995), car boot sales (Gregson and Crewe, 1997) music festivals, alternative rituals and political demonstrations often based around new social movements and New Age beliefs, street markets, popular music festivals, large carnivals, and run-down estates and parks. These spaces, like ruins, exist in the interstices of the city, belonging to a 'wild zone' which resists ordering. The wild zone is a 'contingent site of occupation and colonisation which avoids the objective processes of ordered territorialisation' (Stanley, 1996: 37), a space 'where aesthetics and ethics merge and where there are no defined boundaries and constant ruptures in terms of value' (ibid.: 38).

Interstitial spaces and occasions of the city thus remain, and are also found in its back streets, night-time wastelands and illegal parties; for the size and the actual social diversity of the city means that total order is an impossible goal, and new practices and groups are always coming into existence in other places to disrupt dreams of a regulated world. In addition, despite their intentions, the organising technologies which police and regulate space themselves produce less ordered space, for as Amin and Thrift maintain, the identifiable objectives and the forms of knowledge which are applied create 'gaps, blind spots, mistakes, unreliable paradoxes, ambiguities, anomalies, invisibilities which can only be partially taken in, since they are, to an extent, one of the means by which knowledge itself is created and justified' (2002: 92).

Moreover, the modern counter-tendency to seek the contingent and the unregulated is aptly served by continual change, and the acceleration of transformative
social and cultural processes, wherein modernity is a 'maelstrom of perpetual disintegration and renewal, of struggle and contradiction, of ambiguity and anguish'
(Berman, 1982: 15). Especially under contemporary conditions, the dynamic qualities of an ever-expanding, globalising modernity mean that the diversity of plan-
etary flows further undermine attempts to bound and order space. The city is
perpetually open for business with its spreading, increasingly porous boundaries
and the ways in which it is enfolded into multiple networks. The site of inter-
weaving and disjunctive multiple flows of people, money, information, goods and
technologies (Appadurai, 1990), extending locally and globally, the city is continually reconstituted as a concatenation of heterogeneous processes, temporalities
and sites in a state of becoming and fluidity. This endless urban flux thwarts
attempts to order space and fix it within a matrix of predictable networks, despite
efforts to capture flows and define an urban essence. On occasion, the illusion of
fixity may pertain for a while so that urban rhythms and spaces are stitched
together in routinised, persistent patterns, but this is always subject to change.

The dynamic tendency of capitalist modernity is particularly geared to the production of surplus, and whilst under most conditions there may be an excess of

possible actions, things to possess, materialities and experiences available, the contemporary city is particularly productive of superabundance. I will discuss the material surfeit found in ruins in the next chapter, but we might consider ruins themselves as exemplary of this surplus. For like the mounds of matter produced through construction which are typically deposited on the outskirts of the city, ruins are excess matter, containing superfluous energy and meaning, which as disorderly intrusions, often in more central areas of the city, always come back to haunt the planners' vision of what the city should be. These excessive spaces and materialities strike a chord with Bataille's idea that production always generates its negative, a formless spatial and material excess which rebukes dreams of unity (1991). For as Neilsen remarks, '(T)he concrete matter of the city will always exceed the ambition and attempts to control and shape it, and will always have features that cannot be exposed in the representations that planning has to work with' (2002: 54).).

As a consequence, there is a profusion of urban resources – spaces, things, meanings – that can be utilised in innumerable ways. This glut reveals the limitations of the commodified, planned city, for as Tagg (1996: 181) observes, urban 'regimes of spectacles and discourses do not work … they are never coherent, exhaustive or closed in the ways they are fantasised as being … they cannot shed that ambivalence which always invades their fixities and unsettles their gaze'. Instead, they are 'crossed over, grafittied, reworked, picked over like a trash heap … plagued by unchannelled mobility and unwarranted consumption that feeds unabashed, on excess in the sign values of commodities'. As we will see, ruins are exemplary spaces that simultaneously produce disorder and semiotic and material excess. They contain manifold unruly resources with which people can construct meaning, stories and practices.

To draw together some of these arguments about the ongoing production of urban order and disorder, and to prefigure the discussion about the disorderly effects of ruins, I want to consider briefly Michel Foucault's notion of *heterotopia* (1986), which is, as Lees (1997) points out, a highly suggestive but obscure and underdetermined notion. Foucault affirms that modern processes of classifying knowledge and drawing boundaries between spheres, spaces and categories of all kinds are thwarted by the inevitable eruptions of ambiguity and transparency into the arbitrary distinctions that consign things, places and people to discrete realms. For instance, Lees uses the example of the library to show how the categorisation of texts simultaneously contains infinite multitudes of difference. Since the library conjures up and is related to innumerable other spaces and temporalities which it juxtaposes in a single space, the confined space it appears to be explodes into infinitudes. Thus through the very processes of modernity, there is always likely to be the inadvertent production of heterotopias. In addition to this, however, heterotopia may also have parallels with places and spaces which are organised more loosely, in contingent fashion, perhaps marginally and over limited spells of time, where peculiar juxtapositions of objects and spaces seems disorderly, where hybrids and amalgamations are the rule, elements which rebuke the normative modern orderings and encodings of space. Here, heterotopia is an unrepresentable space 'whose very otherness disturbs speech and dissolves myths … (in which) limits are shattered and language is brought to the threshold of impossibility' (Stanley, 1996: 43). Ruins are exemplary spaces of this sort of heterotopia. The affective, peculiar sensations experienced in the ruin slip away from those normative procedures through which space is represented and categorised. Through the disruptive, performative embodiment of passing through a ruin, and the imposition of space comprising 'a concrete and sensuous concatenation of material forces' (Wylie, 2002: 251), the difficulty of detaching oneself dislocates the tendency to classify and categorise experiences.

Ruins and their Phantom Networks

In order to explore ordering processes further, I now look at how urban bureaucracies, industries and communities of all sorts try to retain their solidity and continuity by maintaining the constituent links which bind their projects together. Similarly I want to consider the ways in which the constellations of people, energy, technology, material, spaces and money are enrolled to sustain and, more crucially, order the factory, and then show how these regulating processes are ruined and thenceforth evoke a shadow of order.

In recent times, the increasingly widespread uses of metaphors of networks and flows have been mobilised, to explain the social as something that involves the enrolment of things and non-human forms of life to achieve order. The relationality of all these networked elements and the ways in which they are stitched into the network bestows upon them a stable character. In addition, these accounts have acted to further Massey's (1993) notion that places are not fixed, essential or identifiable entities but are instead composed of numerous associations, and moreover, places can be considered as being usually enfolded into various networks stretched out through different time-spaces. The securing of specific spatial identities at different scales – based around industry, place-image or other local cultural characteristics – involves the sustenance of these networks. Thus these insights about networks and the characteristics of place have been vital in understanding processes of social ordering. For social, economic and political order is assembled by the tethering together of a host of flows, of capturing and maintaining increasingly global flows of money and materials, people, information and expertise, and rendering these flows reliable and consistent. A defining characteristic of contemporary power is to be able to consolidate these flows – though this can be difficult since they are highly disjunctive and uneven (Appadurai, 1990) – for as long as

possible, or to be able to rapidly reconstitute and reassemble new constellations of flows in different spaces over time. This process of continually ordering and reordering social space passes through spells of heightened volatility where whole networks are reassembled in different parts of the world, through which they are increasingly stretched across ever greater operational scales. The production of ruins can be considered as one of the outcomes of this endless reconstitution of gathering materials, humans, money and ideas together, part of the excess of capitalist production outlined above.

During a productive era, factory owners and managers try to maintain a consistent upkeep of space through time. Industrial infrastructure emerges through a sewing together of a vast network of heterogeneous associations within a productive complex. By conscripting tools, materials, labour and other elements, specific interactions can be institutionalised and extended through space and time. The factory may thus constitute a localised nodal point in a network – that larger entity which frames its practical conventions and procedures – or if large, it may also be a central node which powerfully acts to consolidate the network and recruit far-flung processes into its orbit. At whatever scale, local production is enabled with the flows of objects, people, money, expertise, management, materials and tech-nology which are brought into the factory from far and wide. Similarly, products and money are subsequently sent forth from the factory into the world along estab-lished channels via transport, advertising, retail and wholesale networks across space and time. The sheer scale of the maintenance of the networked flows which render production reliable and stable is difficult to perceive, given that it involves innumerable entrenched and habitual practices which are enacted at multiple scales and institutionalised in many locations, but it enables established activities to carry on ticking over. Nevertheless, flows that surround the factory are densest at the local level and thinner as they stretch away from the local context. Thus, though not necessarily crucial to the survival of the larger network, a particular sense of the local emerges out of the existence of industrial production at a site over time, and is embodied and realised through this concentration of flows. And part of this local dimension – what secures the local – is the situated maintenance of order, of holding the local components of the network in place and ensuring their connection to the wider entity. To make sense of the diverse ways in which places temporarily cohere or disassemble, Mol and Law (1994) have proffered three spatialities which they identify as 'region', 'network' and 'fluid'. In an indus-trial context, 'regions' are akin to the stable arrangements whereby suppliers, workers, transporters, materials, wholesalers and so on are sewn into the infra-structure which maintains local industrial production. 'Networks' extend these various local connections across wider spatialities to incorporate international markets, materials and supply lines within a globally constituted corporate enter-prise, thus folding factories into this wider context. 'Fluid' spaces are typified by much looser arrangements wherein the enrolment of places and people into rela-tionships tends to be much more volatile, unstable and contingent. Connections are multiple and shifting, at variance to the ordered stabilities of the region and the network. The ruined factory then, can be characterised as existing within this fluid state, its future uncertain, whereas it was once more evidently situated within a dense assemblage of regional connections and incorporated into a wider, more stable network.

The sustenance of networks in an everyday sense also depends upon what Ingold and Kurttila (2000) describe as 'taskscapes': everyday spaces that are fos-tered by the ways in which habits and habitation recreate local and domestic space and render it comfortable and homely, the unquestioned backdrop to daily tasks, pleasures and routine movement. A taskscape is necessarily organised to enable continuity and stability so that quotidian manoeuvres and modes of dwelling come to be unreflexively carried out, consolidating a practical disposition amongst workers and bosses of how to work and behave. This conceptualisation of place is that it 'exists through the realisable projects and availabilities, patterns of use and users, all of which are practically negotiated daily' and embodied by habituated subjects (ibid.: 90–1). Spatial constraints and opportunities inhere in the qualities of places and these mesh with the bodily dispositions emerging out of the routine practices of its inhabitants that become embedded over time. Despite the apparent stability of such arrangements, grounded in habit and unreflexive practice, the dynamism of global capitalism is always liable to render them obsolete, thereby shattering the taskscape and the space it produces.

In the factory and its surrounds, the relationships which restrain the meanings of things are laid out in space. People perform everyday tasks by moving across space, and around fixtures, following procedures and using particular objects in particular places at particular times, such fixtures constraining other possibilities as well as providing stages upon which to enact normative work routines. The industrial process generally relies upon the idea that an object must pass between different stages of production, each located in discrete spaces which are connected to each other as part of a sequence. Most basically, raw materials are imported, processed, shaped, finished and packaged in separate processes in separate spaces. Thus the stabilisation of relations between the things, people and machines belonging to one part of the shop floor intimately depend upon their relations with other spaces which precede and follow them in the sequence of production, and also implicitly with more distant parts of the wider network into which the factory is installed. In the following chapter, I will discuss the ways in which the material world of objects is ordered so that things are kept 'in place' and are quickly restored to their position when it is believed that they are 'out of place'.

In the ruin, these sequences of productive action reliant on the organisation of time, space and materiality are now absent. For abandoned factories suddenly lose their position in the networks which render their meaning and function stable, as the complex infrastructure which surrounds the operation of an industrial site comes apart. Suddenly detached from these enduring sets of heterogeneous associations, entirely sidelined from a network or perhaps only possessing residual connection – for instance, as corporate real estate – the ruin loses its former purpose and meaning. This removal of a local site from a wider network usually means the conscription of other locales so that heterogeneous materials, people, and places through – for instance, the transfer of production to East Asia – become enmeshed within the network. Or else the network may wither or fragment, with certain constellations and flows grafted onto new networks. Accordingly, as the ruined factory becomes disconnected from the wider multiple flows out of which it originated, including the local connections which held it in place, it is spatially recontextualised by devolving back into a set of different local associations, a disembedding followed by a contingent and temporary re-embedding. For as discussed in the previous chapter, it becomes enrolled into new human and non-human networks, although the social and cultural practices which forge such webs tend to be less concerned with the maintenance of order, operate more contingently and are always precarious given the transformed status of the ruin as superfluous entity.

In the factory, great patterns of mundane, quotidian scheduling are necessary to ensure the timely arrival and departure of goods, people and money. Machines and other fixtures are sited in rooms which are then defined by their purpose and these specialised spaces are organised as interlinked stages to accommodate a sequence of activities through which products are processed, administered and despatched. The repetition of routines, tasks and procedures over time consolidates the spatialised order of production, securing the ontological resonance of the network further, and imposing rhythms (Lefebvre, 1996) upon the denizens of the factory through the allocation of clock discipline and other codes. Hierarchies are equally stamped onto space, typically with boardrooms and offices situated on higher floors and supervisory rooms placed to survey the shop floor below. There are thus clearly assigned and separate spaces for unskilled and skilled workers, supervisory staff such as foremen, office workers, managers and board members. In addition, disciplinary infrastructures impose monthly targets for production, alert workers to rules and regulations, establish punitive procedures if these rules are breached, offer rewards for specific acts and negative consequences for the failure to be efficient. Factories also contain numerous notices which remind workers about the correct procedures: those banning forbidden activities, insisting on proper and responsible behaviour, instructing in the necessary methods for operating machinery, identifying points for congregation and drawing attention to the factory bylaws.

Ruined factories are replete with the traces of this redundant power, poignant reminders of the ordering functions necessary for the maintenance of industrial networks. There is something comical about these remaining signatures of hierarchy and authority. Like the strident orders barked out by a solitary sergeant major in the middle of a deserted space, no one is there to listen and obey. The trivial warnings and commands to follow procedures seem ridiculous outbursts of petty authority. The signs of production with its sequential order become elliptical as walls erode and rooms appear to be at the centre of formless labyrinths, and no longer do social barriers to progression through these spaces pertain. All are equal in their status as ruined and decaying spaces, and the careful distinctions between rooms which were designed to demarcate hierarchical arrangements and specific functions become meaningless. The foremen's huts situated above the shop floor collapse and join the space in which workers toiled. The boardroom, stripped of furniture, is just another empty and rotting room.

The effusion of detritus and the disarray of displaced things reveals that there are no longer any vital functions of continual restoration. There are no longer any cleaners, floor polishers, store room workers, brooms and repainting jobs; no army of mops and buckets that descend upon the factory when the rest of the working day ceases. This also reminds us that one of the most vital yet unrecognised signs of mundane ordering is the work that goes into keeping decay and non-human intrusion at bay, in keeping out damp and spraying weedkiller. And besides this, the channels which formerly sustained the connections enabling the smooth operation of industrial production are truncated and clogged up. The conduits through which electricity, water, transport-borne goods and materials, people, information, heat and light announce their curtailment by their current state. Water and heating pipes are stripped of cladding and broken, perhaps dripping onto floors. Electric wiring is severed, splaying out from its confines behind plaster or tube. Sewers and water courses are bunged up with rubble and blocked off, phones lie off the hook and detached from connections, roads and rail exits disappear under banks of earth, radiators and lights are smashed and disconnected.

Besides the disordering of factory maintenance, the eloquent testimony of mute objects reveals that the objects manufactured or stored in the factory have also suddenly been dropped from the network through which they were made and

circulated. These networks into which they were installed defined their use and meaning, but this may evaporate with this detachment. Would-be commodities spill across floors, lie dormant in loading bays, on conveyor belts, awaiting obliteration or reinterpretation and reuse, or incorporation in other networks of meaning. Boxes are piled up for export but will never be sent, chits and receipts lie across office space never to be filed, sour milk lies in the fridge, never to be drunk. Incomplete parts will never be attached to other pieces or elaborated upon, unfinished artefacts will never be burnished and polished so that they can be sold as finished products, and indeed such objects are often unidentifiable in their formerly partial but now complete state. Even if they have been finished, objects may be useless now that they have become detached from commodity flows and, as I will discuss in the next chapter, are frequently indecipherable.

Whilst such networked connections may be suddenly dropped from local environs, they remain partially in place, for the workers' habits and their recent memories of doing and being in place are likely to fade only gradually. Thus these connections are stored in memory but also articulated in the friendships, leisure practices and temporal routines to which workers became habituated over the years of employment. Moreover, if employed for many years, and especially if the form of employment was manual, bodies will have been partly shaped by the repetitive

tasks undertaken. However, these social traces of the network have been muted and are mostly invisible in the space of the ruin now that they are detached from the larger framework of activity and meaning.

Besides the demise of ordering functions within these buildings, the outside of factories were also regulated. Car parks and roads were swept clean of dirt and subject to the spraying of weedkiller to limit the intrusions of plants. Typically, a more orderly confinement of vegetation was organised around the maintenance of lawns, trees, verges, flower beds and shrubbery so that a green environment surrounded those factories built in the second half of the twentieth century. Following the strictures laid down by models of suitable gardening in the archetypes of park design and the bourgeois garden, such landscaping generally followed the aesthetics of a restrained and regulated nature. Comprising manicured lawns and verges, the ongoing pruning of stray vegetation and the maintenance of separate areas bordered by hedges, flower beds and kerbs, the garden mirrored the orderly segmentation of space within the factory. In addition, the selection of specific kinds of plants – deemed suitable to give a certain hue and shape – provided a pleasing splash of colour, although the functionality of the factory is rarely disrupted by startling or remarkable natural forms, conforming to the conversion of nature into manageable spaces which require low maintenance and conform to regular geometric designs.

Of course, these imperatives of form and function are traduced by the outgrowths and invasions that become profuse when the factory becomes abandoned. Formerly confined forms of plant life violate the boundaries which kept them in check, growing over, through or around barriers. The policing of intrusive plants vanishes and weeds may strangle and suffocate the chosen flora, so that new species colonise the previously kempt flower beds. In the absence of pruning, some plants grow huge and burst out of the restraints imposed by their cultivated form. Lawns become indistinguishable as grass grows and a wide variety of plants sink roots into this newly wild space. Pruned and carefully separated plants in rose beds grow and merge into great and impenetrable bushes, hedges spread out, and ornamental grasses and plants break through the pots which contained them and thrust their roots into the evolving cracks of the tarmac or paving on which they were sited. Other plants wither and die, or are overshadowed by faster growing varieties. Certain seed-dispersing plants colonise quickly, sending out their progeny to colonise other parts of the garden and the interior of the factory, further blurring the formerly well-kept distinction between outside and inside. Saplings cleave walls and pavements apart.

As I have observed, the quick colonisation and transformation of formerly cultivated space through this unconfined growth means that derelict sites may become particularly problematic when they spill out of their boundaries, beyond the boarded windows and fences that confine them. Plants are apt to jettison their wind-borne seeds across the city and animals move out of their nest and dens to prowl the world beyond the ruin. Here nature can be a desirable interruption in the urban fabric, where a fox leaves its den in a former landscaped garden to cross local gardens or an owl flies out from its nest in a decaying attic to hoot in the night. Yet where other species such as rats and giant hogweed move out of derelict spaces, they provoke fear that the urban is becoming threatened by an unruly nature. As mentioned in the previous chapter, feral cats provoke a range of responses which highlight the ambivalences of a nature that transgresses the assigned boundaries between urban and rural (Griffiths, Poulter and Sibley, 2000). They provoke further confusion since it is not clear whether they can be categorised as domestic or wild. Accordingly, they may be conceived of as out of place and worthy of extermination as pests, or regarded as in need of rescue from the deprivation of the wild. Alternatively, they are cared for and welcomed as different sorts of urban dwellers who bring life to the city but this may be dependent upon the spaces they move across: if they keep to their derelict sites there may be no problem, but if they venture into suburbia they may be more threatening.

This rampant exploitation of derelict space reveals that nature is not separate but will always ignore previous attempts to maintain boundaries between culture and nature, and will thwart the assignation of plants and animals to specific ecological niches or to agricultural, domestic or 'wild' domains (Philo and Wilbert, 2000). To reinforce the point made earlier, despite the systematic forms of regulation which try to minimise intrusions from non-human life, all urban sites are subject to the agency of non-humans who improvise and adapt to places, and transform their behaviours and habits in response to constraints and opportunities. For animals and plants are parts of networks which are rarely confined to singular spaces but, like humans, are constantly on the lookout to discover new places in which to dwell and use. The colonisation of ruins makes it apparent that non-humans are enmeshed with human spaces and interactions; they can only partially be assigned to separate realms and only then for a duration dependent upon the maintenance of strategies to delimit spatial fixity.

The Disorderly Aesthetics of Ruins

The aesthetic ordering of the city involves the continual maintenance and scrupulous restoration of surfaces, their cleansing and their cladding with material imbued with smooth textures. Urban reinvention requires that old buildings in city centres and 'heritage' areas are sandblasted and retiled, and that adjacent areas become equipped with street furniture. Similarly, the colour coding of urban space tends to assemble pastel and mineral shades to compose a muted theme, and this is offset by the brighter intrusion of colour in the commercial districts through the blare of window displays and adverts. The textural consistencies of walls and paving, notably in central areas, are thus smoothed by constant cleansing and painting, and especially where they are identifiably old, restored so as to obliterate the patina which tells of degenerative ageing. Within such regimes of urban resurfacing, the interruptions of daubed slogans and fly-posters are an intolerable rebuke to the manufactured seamlessness. Where these illusory attempts to arrest the depredations of time require vigilance, environmental vicissitudes in ruins are accelerated by neglect so that processes of decomposition prematurely age the fabric. Unfamiliar and hugely varied textures emerge when the armies of renovators are not required; and former strategies to maintain shiny, flat surfaces are defeated by the dynamic agency of mould, damp and chemistry. Erupting through the last coat are a random collection of earlier layers, as paint bubbles and blisters, cracks open to reveal a combination of coverings comprising primer, undercoat or whitewash. At a later stage of decay, other materials are presented to produce variable mixtures of cracking plaster, sections of wallpaper, bricks, lath, timber and concrete. These festoons of ornamentation comprising bubbles, cracks, peelings, emergent mould, random discolourings, and the residues deposited by water, create a patina that is at variance to the smoothed-over façades of renovated buildings and deliberately distressed surfaces of commodities which masquerade as

antique. Contrastingly, this testifies to an ageing process that – rather than fabricated or arrested – seems to be hastened. These textural medleys are accompanied by remnants of wooden notice boards, fractured electrical sockets, rusty nails and various other scraps and adorned with green shocks of moss, lichen and cobwebs. Moreover, shadows create unfamiliar patterns on walls and floors as removed sections of roof, sprouting vegetation and hanging wires and artefacts cast their impressions across brick and concrete. These spaces are dis-ordered by the agency of non-human life forms which seek out opportunities for spreading and colonising, and by the contingencies of climate.

The notion that space should be divided up to prevent different elements from mingling is part of the normative aesthetic ordering of space, a modernist aesthetic regulation replete with design codes purporting to embody common-sense notions through which 'appropriate' visual appearance masquerades as objectively correct. These codes are embodied in the modernisms of the international style, with their preference for right angles and the erasure of ornament. Influential architects such as Le Corbusier (1995) and Loos (see Hughes, 1980) berate the presence of decoration as decadent, primitive, uncivilised and excremental, and urban landscapes are best where there are uncluttered vistas. Although such ideas about architecture and design are now routinely derided, they articulate the primacy placed upon the

spacing of functions, buildings and things so as to foster the evolution of a healthy 'modern' subject whose brain is uncluttered by irrelevant distractions which linger in the common-sense assumptions of much contemporary urban planning. And although the era of high modernism embodied by the international style has passed, similar injunctions about appropriate spacings endure in postmodern landscapes, and in the advice about aesthetics dished out in lifestyle programmes concerned with garden and home refurbishment (Brunsdon, 2003).

Such regimes of ordering require that objects in a space should relate to each other in particular ways, should neither be too close nor distant from each other. Colours should be generally unblemished and distinct, generally somewhat muted or pastel-coloured, except where a bright colour provides a counterpoint to the general tone or is utilised to highlight a particular feature or function. Domestic and work places seem to be subject to ever more rigorous codes that attempt to establish harmony through space, so that all elements should conform to a general design. Specialist designers are called in to shape such space, and fixtures, colours and the arrangement of objects are subordinate to this overall theme. This grand aesthetic coding can be witnessed across urban space as shopping centres, streets and even whole districts are subject to makeovers which attribute and express their identity through design. Specific 'heritage' areas, with apparent 'historic', 'regional' characteristics and styles are policed to ensure buildings conform to specifications about which kinds of structures, building materials, colours and ornamentation are allowed, so that the 'tone' of a place may be maintained, often fixing a place within a scrubbed-up version of a particular historical era. Where difference features in aesthetically themed space, it is not allowed to stick out like a sore thumb but must be refashioned in accordance with visual and textural norms. Alternatively, a little soupçon of difference might be regarded as enticing for shoppers and tourists but is carefully contextualised within the overall design.

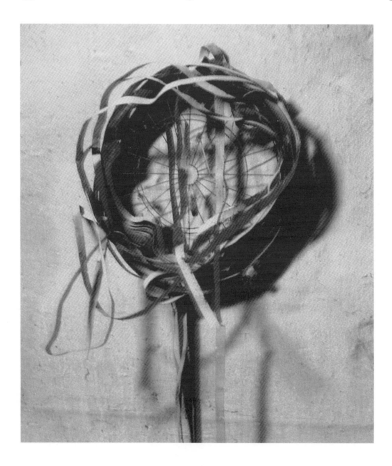

Unusual objects are displayed in ways akin to the exhibition of objects in museums, in that they are decontextualised by their positioning which highlights their exclusivity and their excludedness from the wider space. Similarly, window displays situate separate commodities in isolation. Rarely multiple or mixed, such objects and images are confined and tamed. The ongoing reproduction of aestheticised space includes overt and more subtle policing which views other, more glaring intrusions into this landscape as threateningly unsightly and symptomatic of fears about potential disorder – well beyond a simple transgression of visual order – and meld with concerns about status maintenance, crime, the threat of strangers, property values and so on. Interruptions in themed space such as graffiti or bill-posting are routinely depicted as signs of anti-social behaviour and disrespect, despite the alternative information and vitality they might connote. So too are offences such as painting a door the 'wrong' colour, allowing a hedge to grow too high or using inappropriate building materials, for in suburbia and city centres such assumed violations are accused of 'letting the neighbourhood down'.

Ruins entirely rebuke these normative aesthetic orderings and accordingly are ubiquitously described as unattractive or ugly. My own view is that, conversely, they gain an aesthetic charge by virtue of this difference, in that their disruption of these conventions is evident in markedly alternative sights which simultaneously highlight the enforced semiotics of space. The aesthetic customs of form, beauty, placing and display are reframed in the ruin. At once, the ever-present illumination of all urban interior space, whether through the electric light which penetrates all corners or the natural light which floods through windows, is *not* present. There are dark places to move into, places in which the eyes must become accustomed to the vague shapes within the gloom. This experience of darkness is unusual enough and is complemented by the play of light and shade throughout. On sharp, bright days, peculiar shadows stretch along walls, and sunlight pours through fractured roofs, creating complex, uneven geometric patterns across floors, although sudden changes in the weather might suddenly dispel these strongly etched mosaics of light. All dimensions, from the roof to the floors to the walls, are subject to processes of degeneration and gradually give up their surface sheen. Unexpected juxtapositions of objects offer disorganised scenes, and an abundance of hybrid forms deny the designed separation of colours, objects and textures, providing an alternative aesthetics of dissonance and peculiar associations. Confounding the axes of verticality and horizontality, and the continued primacy of the right angle so beloved of Le Corbusier and his modernist architectural adherents, the ruin presents a funhouse of the skew-whiff and the oblique. The decidedly un-curated things within this askew spatiality testify to the force of their own agency in their reconstituted state and position, as well as that of the weather and of other life-forms and of the components of the buildings in which they are housed, as I will discuss in greater detail in the following chapter.

Unlike artistic and commercial montage, ruins contain not deliberately organised assemblies devised to strike chords and meanings through associations, but fortuitous combinations which interrupt normative meanings. The placement of objects into a montage 'interrupts the context into which it has been inserted', counteracting the illusion of ordered normality (Buck-Morss, 1989: 67). The assemblages forged in the window display, the museum cabinet, the interior design and the advertisement are part of a 'conscious principle of construction', through which utopian wish-images about the reordering of the world are converted into the fetishisation of objects through commodificiation (ibid.:74). These artful montages disguise difference 'by fusing the elements so artfully that all evidence of incompatibility and contradiction, indeed, all evidence of artifice, is eliminated' from the display (ibid.). Such encoded arrangements thus organise things within spaces, creating patterns which claim normativity as part of the mundane and systematic production of the spectacular and ornamental. The happenstance montages of ruined space, however, comment both ironically on the previously fixed meanings of their constituent objects, and the ever-so-carefully arranged montages of commodified space. Pleasurable by virtue of the interaction between objects bearing different semiotic charges, and the arbitrary relationships between different forms, shapes, textures and materialities, the unending diversity of unencoded material juxtapositions stimulate ineffable sensations. These are connected

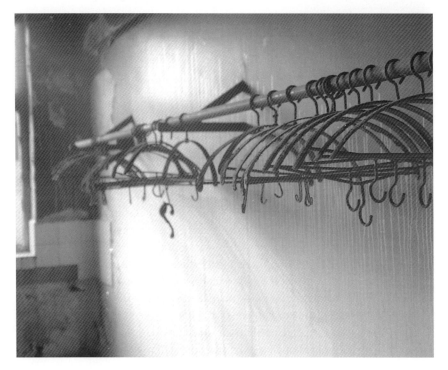

to the variable materiality and tactility of the world, and the surplus meanings which emerge from unexpected conjoinings. By virtue of their arbitrariness and the evident lack of design in the distribution of objects in space, it is difficult to describe the aesthetics of ruins, to recoup such scenes back into dominant systems of representation. And in the ruin, this disorderly displacement and the arbitrary, mysterious appearance of certain objects in places where they clearly do not belong can confound and surprise.

Walking across the vast shop floor of a chain factory in ruins, I pushed open a door to enter a narrow, long chamber. Inside was a conveyor belt, tilted at an angle of forty-five degrees, which carried chains up into a raised compartment about eight feet above the floor, to coat them liberally with lubricating oil, before they descended down the sloping belt on the other side to be stacked for export. Now static, the belt was sprinkled with debris, including chains that were never sent forth for lubrication, and the oil housed in the large, raised basin had congealed to form a dense, coagulating mass akin to a tar pit. For some reason, I wanted to look inside the oiling booth and because the conveyor belt was thick with muck, I placed a long, stout plank at right angles to it and climbed up. After making sure I gained a sound footing, I glanced towards the glutinous basin and was hit with a wave of shock and nausea upon seeing what appeared to be a dead child inert and

floating. Gathering my senses, I gasped for air and moved closer to realise with profound relief that in fact, I was looking at the inflatable dummy of an 'alien', a toy with large eyes which mocked my initial horror. But how on earth had an object such as this found its way into this rather inaccessible piece of apparatus in a deserted and derelict factory? I could only conjecture.

Performance and Sensation in Ruined Space

As briefly discussed above, urban order is also maintained through the pervasive influence of what Foucault (1977) terms 'biopolitics', the instantiation of appro- priate behaviour via normative codes and practices, from notions about the proper comportment of one's body in urban space to the management of sensual experi-

ence through the valorisation of certain senses. I will discuss the production of these embodied conventions before going on to explore how the act of visiting ruins might disrupt and reveal the arbitrariness of their normalisation, offering the potential to experience a rich range of performative and sensual experiences.

The ways in which we move through the city are generally part of that everyday practice through which unreflexive, routinised sequences of movement are performed. The production of these embodied forms of practical knowledge engenders patterns of communal association and a sense of dwelling (Seamon, 1979: 58–9). The co-ordinated, collective patterns created by these everyday, habitual gestures and movements are described by David Seamon as 'place ballets', inscribed upon locales to constitute a compendium of regular and routinised dances. Whether the repetitive movements of gendered tasks or the monotonous work undertaken by factory workers, such choreographies have been compared to the patterns of migratory birds as 'they trace and retrace the same restricted set of options' (MacDonald, 1997: 153).

Since these routines are repetitive, they tend to reinforce notions about what constitutes the common-sense and the unquestioned, and hence provide a bulwark against questioning seemingly intractable conventions, although there are occasions when they may be challenged. The inscription of individual and collective paths then, provides an everyday, normative way of being in the world: 'from the embodiment of habit a consistency is given to the self which allows for the end of doubt' (Harrison, 2000: 503) and, moreover, consolidates the parameters of identity. Internalised and ingrained through interaction with others, habits organise life for individuals, linking them to groups so that 'cultural community is often established by people together tackling the world around them with familiar manoeuvres' (Frykman and Löfgren, 1996: 10–11). These shared habits strengthen affective and cognitive links, consolidate a sense of shared natural habits and *doxa* to constitute a habitus, including acquired skills which minimise unnecessary reflection every time a decision is required, as 'a way to economise on life' (Frykman and Löfgren, 1996: 10).

If we consider these routines as partly constitutive of the normative flows of people within the city and thus productive of particular experiences and sensations, we can see how they trace the performative and spatial conventions which order space. For instance it is commonly argued that in the contemporary city, the body has become 'primarily a performing self of appearance, display and impression management' (Csordas, 1994: 2). Whether collectively or individually, the adoption of stylised postures, gaits and facial expressions, together with codes embodied in clothing, can be considered as choreographed performances through which people communicate meaning. The notion that urbanites perform in space also conjures up the idea that forms of urban space can be considered as stages, and that the nature of the stage encourages specific kinds of performances, enactions which, in turn, reproduce the stage. Indeed, David Harvey describes the postmodern city, with its proliferating signs and settings, as akin to a 'theatre, a series of stages upon which individuals could work their own distinctive magic while performing a multiplicity of roles' (1989: 5).

The nature of urban stages varies from the carefully managed arena which contains discretely situated objects around which performance is organised, to those theatres with blurred boundaries, or those cluttered with other actors following incomprehensible scripts, full of shifting scenes, juxtapositions and random movements coming from a range of angles. Whilst urban stages are inevitably incorporated into multiple, overlapping spaces, and subject to contestation by performers, I want to argue that the city is increasingly composed out of highly regulated stages which constrain the range of performances and experiences. More specifically, the design of cities foregrounds the ability to move seamlessly through space whether as a pedestrian or passenger. Such smooth passage is materialised in the way in which urban space is increasingly organised to facilitate directional movement by both pedestrians and vehicles, by reducing points of entry and exit and minimising idiosyncratic distractions. Marc Augé claims that such designs, instead of being 'relational, historical and concerned with identity' (1995: 107–8), produce realms of 'transit' as opposed to 'dwelling', sites of 'interchange' rather than a meeting place or 'crossroads', where 'communication (with its codes, images and strategies)' is practised rather than affective and convivial language. Thus the flows of people through the city, and hence their potential for enacting varied performances and being subjected to rich experiences, are minimised as they are organised to surge through specific conduits (Cresswell, 1997b). Similarly architecture may well function as a 'potential stimulus for movement, real or imagined' in that 'a building is an incitement to action, a stage for movement and interaction' (Yudell, 1977: 59) with a wealth of possible niches, paths, stairs, openings, tactile surfaces which invite physical exploration. However the channelling of movement, together with the conventions which influence performance within buildings, acts to delimit this potential.

Despite these regulatory systems, Michel de Certeau (1984) famously talks of the ways in which pedestrians tactically forge individual paths through the city's carceral networks, creating contingent 'spaces of enunciation' which evade the strategies of the powerful. This creative inscription is necessarily fleeting but defies attempts to fix and rationalise space. The 'rhetoric of walking', through which pedestrians 'compose a path', clashes with the ordered meanings and pathways etched into the city, although these improvisations are generally confined to 'the chance offerings of the moment', seized on the wing. Other kinds of movement

undermine dominant spatial meanings and render incoherent the logic of official functions and modes of circulation and exchange. For instance, Kawash describes how the movement of the homeless body 'is mapped according to the exigencies of bodily functions' as it searches for places to sleep, keep warm, eat, rest, beg and excrete (Kawash, 1998: 333). Likewise, the *flâneur* can be appropriated as a figure who uncovers the experiences of the unheard, creating alternative narratives of the city, defamiliarising the commonplace and celebrating the unfamiliar and carnivalesque (Jenks and Neves, 2000: 4). In addition to these disordering movements, alternative spatial networks evolve 'in the interstitial spaces between dominant orderings' (Stanley, 1996), along the cracks between regulated spaces. The presence of these marginal spaces such as ruins, which produce a blurring of boundaries and 'constant ruptures in terms of value' (ibid.), provide unfamiliar contexts

for more improvised performances which respond to chance meetings and contingent events and facilitate the enaction of different pathways.

As mentioned above, urban spatialisation and the inculcation of performative and sensory norms impinges upon the sensual experience of the city, for as Feld notes, 'as place is sensed, senses are placed; as places make sense, senses make place' (1996: 91). Thus ways of sensing are partly produced out of 'a shared world of intermundane space which crosses over and intertwines with that of similarly embodied human beings' (Williams and Bendelow, 1998: 53) through inter-corporeal relations. As Casey (2001) outlines, place is apprehended by means of habitus, through habitation and via incorporation into the body, and this is partly achieved through the production of a series of habitual enactions through what I earlier called the 'taskscape'. The taskscape foregrounds unreflexive modes of dwelling, of being-in-the-world, of mundanely organising and sensing the environment of familiar space. The operation of the senses is thus central to understanding the interplay between people and space. Here then is a situated, sensuous engagement with the environment; one which continuously emerges out of an unfixed and improvisatory disposition, which nevertheless is influenced by conventions and traditional practice. Such sensual, knowledgeable practices make space and are part of the ways in which people inhabit space and come to belong in it.

The senses are thus 'cumulative and accomplished, rather than given' (Stewart, 1999: 18) and do not provide an unmediated access to the world as purely 'natural' tools. For ways of conceptualising senses are imbued with cultural values, hence the prioritisation given to sight in Western modernity: 'sensory values not only frame a culture's experience, they express its ideals, its hopes and its fears' (Claessen, 1993: 136), its social relations, its cultural practices and its forms of practical living. For instance, smell can justify 'not only essentialist views of inferior or superior places, but also desirable and undesirable people' (Drobnick, 2002: 37). Senses are conditioned via cultural, practical techniques and conventions of being in the world; they also rely upon the affordances of the space they move through. As Seremetakis puts it, 'the sensory is not only encapsulated within the body as an internal capacity or power but is also dispersed out there on the surface of things as the latter's autonomous characteristics, which can then invade the body as perceptual experience' (1994: 6). Affordances thus inform a practical engagement which becomes part of 'second nature' where people are familiar with space.

To return to the contemporary city and its propensity to produce sensual experiences, Richard Sennett (1994: 15) argues that urban space has largely become 'a mere function of motion', engendering a 'tactile sterility' where the city environment 'pacifies the body'. The imperative to minimise disruption and distraction for pedestrians and drivers means that movement is typified by rapid transit without arousal. In the case of the car, the physical efforts – the 'micro-movements' – used to negotiate space are minimal, producing a desensitised effect. Indeed, although the 'desire to move freely' has been realised by those with enough time and money, this 'has triumphed over the sensory claims of the space through which the body moves'. This speed of movement through the city is conducive to the formation of an 'image repertoire' through which moving people can quickly distinguish between signs that indicate points of attraction and direction, picking out informative signifiers like traffic signs, shop logos and advertisements. Accordingly, the sensations of the city are dominated by the visual in accordance with the requirements of producers of simulations and spectacles.

This form of urban movement and spectacularisation is also captured by Trevor Boddy's (1992) term, the 'analogous city', which describes a set of 'new urban prosthetics', a system of smooth and sealed walkways, escalators, bridges, people-conveyors and tunnels. Escalators and moving walkways are designed according to very specific notions of 'efficiency', controlling the direction and the pace of pedestrians' movement, leading them to desirable sites or past designated sights, restricting physical communication and adjustment. Constituting a comprehensive movement system to link work, recreational and commercial spaces, these systems produce an aesthetic and material form typified by 'incessant whirring', 'mechanical breezes', 'vaguely reassuring icons', 'trickling fountains', and anaesthetic qualities like low murmurings and insensate movements. Simulating urbanity but filtering out 'troubling smells and winds', these staged environments segregate classes and ethnicities, and are the scene of a distinct repertoire of bodily expression: 'never a clenched fist, a passionate kiss, a giddy wink, a fixed-shoulder stride' (123–4). As such, these environments are devised to reduce sensual intrusions and interruptions inimical to swift movement and the enaction of consumption-based activities. Like the tourist spaces discussed by Rojek, such designs shut out 'extraneous, chaotic elements' and reduce 'visual and functional forms to a few key images' (1995: 62). By framing views, sights, photograph points and cultures, the visual design of highly commodified and regulated spaces that construct the aesthetic conventions discussed above, direct the gaze but in such a way as to repress the kinaesthetic qualities of vision by removing rich tactile, auditory and aromatic experiences.

The foregrounding of the visual is accompanied, then, by olfactory regulation. The erasure of strong smells, disruptive noises and rough textures produces the 'blandscapes' described by Drobnick, namely those 'aseptic places, created by the modernist drive towards deodorization, that are so empty that they lead to an alienating sense of placelessness' (2002: 34). A disdain for strong smells persists for they continue to signify poverty, disease, decadence and decay, the antitheses of high modernity (see Bauman, 1994: 24), and hence must be confined to particular areas, well away from suburbanites, shopping centres and tourists. Moreover, strong smells transgress 'social conventions in regard to enjoyment, discipline, functionalism, corporeal deportment' (Drobnick, 2002: 35). Similarly, sound is

carefully controlled. Little is permitted to disrupt the calm, toned-down atmosphere which has become synonymous with relaxation, and soundscapes comprising the tinkle of fountains and piped muzak drift through urban spaces whose surfaces are designed to muffle the noise of pedestrians. Tactility is also organised so that smooth surfaces prevail on walls and floors, clutter and dirt are eradicated and evident routes are maintained. The seamlessness of linear movement and the even surfaces of polished floors and paving underfoot mean that the body remains undisturbed in its progress and is able to perform unhindered movement towards destinations.

An ordering repertoire, comprising the production of spectacular, desensitised, functional, commodified, highly staged space – with the persistence of unperformative norms which reiterate how people should behave in the city – pervades the contemporary urban experience and exemplifies the present ascendance of Apollonian modernity in this sphere. However, as I have inferred, other practices and places exist which contrast with these disciplinary regimes and highlight the ways in which they masquerade as the embodiment of common-sense, universal values.

The factory was once the site for highly choreographed and co-ordinated place ballets which emerged from the ordering of production; it was a structured taskscape, in which habitual movements between and across spaces became normative and unreflected upon. In a ruined state, however, there is no longer anybody to supervise movement, no imperative to secure the spatial ordering embodied in performative roles, no fellow workers to survey one's movements, no need for self-consciousness about one's performative competence, and no entrapment within a planned allocation of functional spaces. The site has changed from an intensively managed stage to a disorganised stage.

Instead of moving towards objects and objectives, bodies tend to move arbitrarily in ruins. With the demolition of guided pathways, and social and physical barriers between spaces, as walls and doors collapse, large ruins evolve into a labyrinthine structure which permit the making of a multitude of paths, in contradistinction to the largely linear routes through space determined by processes of production. Thus movement through a ruin is determined by whim or contingency in an improvisational path-making, according to what catches the eye or looks as if it might promise surprises or appears pleasurably negotiable. In the same way that there are no social barriers to movement across space, there are no temporal restrictions that determine how long one should stay in any location, no curbs on loitering and lingering, and no conventions that prevent slow movement or stillness, fostering a freedom over spatial temporalities that can contrast with the fast world outside with its purposive directedness.

Progress through a ruin is comparable to the *dérives* embarked upon by the Situationists, who were characteristically drawn to places on the margins of urban life, such as out of date arcades and fleamarkets. In these locations, sights, characters and artefacts could be found which disturbed the planned and commodified city: unruly and outmoded elements which seemed to lack meaning and were thus charged by their incommensurability with the new and the fashionable. Situationists offered the *dérive* as a technique to bypass and subvert the commodification of everyday space, and the spectacularisation and bureaucratic disciplining of the city (see Knabb, 1981). Instead, the *dérive* advocates a playful abandonment of purposive mobility and encourages the walker to be drawn towards unexpected sights and places beyond hegemonic regulation and representation. Rather than following linear pathways, pedestrians were advised to be influenced by sudden changes of ambience and other non-purposive sentiments and 'irrational' feelings, to 'excavate a network of anti-spectacular spaces' (Sadler, 1998: 92). Characterised by their apparently non-spectacular mundaneness but also by the particular atmospheres which surrounded them, and gleaned through their psychogeographical resonances, they served as exemplary counter-sites from which revolutionary desires and understandings could be articulated. Accordingly, places could be more appropriately conceptualised according to poetic and emotional criteria, so pedestrians would enter the 'Happy Quarter', the 'Bizarre Quarter', the 'Sinister Quarter', or the 'Noble and Tragic Quarter'. This reappraisal jammed the messages imparted by the 'mechanistic functioning of the city' (Sadler, 1998: 91) and consequently revealed the arbitrary absurdities of the well-worn paths which pedestrians follow (Bonnett, 1989). The Situationists hoped that this practical decoding and deconstruction of norms of movement and perception might be replaced by an infinite variety of environments in which liberated bodies might experience diverse encounters.

In terms of the ways in which bodies circulate within ruins, the lack of a centre and the absence of any obvious linear pathways allows a wandering in all directions, which in turn, encourages entry in to a host of spaces not usually designed for bodies or prohibited to all but a few. Thus one can move in and out of machines, slide down chutes, climb up ladders to store rooms and attics, lounge on the boardroom table, go into toilets used by the opposite sex and temporarily dwell in large cupboards. Rather than functional rooms, such spaces seem akin to caves, passages and other archetypal dream spaces. Besides this liberating of the body's movement, other spaces can seem strange and disruptive. In one factory, in a vast first storey denuded of all extraneous fitments, a wooden floor which had been overlaid onto a concrete surface had buckled and warped, because of the effect of the water which flowed onto it when it rained. This resulted in a fantastic and extensive series of regular waves, each with a crest some two feet high, and although static, the diagonal axis of the waves provided a remarkable sight giving the illusory impression of movement. The wooden sea was in some places slippery and thus rather difficult to negotiate, like a funhouse attraction, and necessitated careful manoeuvring. More typically, with the collapse of walls and the evacuation of machinery and other fixtures, sprawling shop floors can present themselves as vast, open spaces with unusually expansive vistas. The body can suddenly become conscious of its situation as a single presence in a vast interior space, made uncanny in its contrast to the closed in perspectives usually offered by interiors cluttered with placed objects and people. And yet this expanse also provides opportunities for hurtling across unpeopled space without being concerned about how we might appear to others.

These possibilities of extravagant passage are engendered by the affordances of the ruin which force the body to bend, stoop, climb, swerve around obstacles, jump and weave. Actually entering a ruin might involve clambering over a wall, forging a path through undergrowth and squeezing one's body through a fractured window, taking care to avoid the glass shards that remain. Exploration might involve a careful treading upon slippery timber, an awareness of loose floorboards or stairs, a reluctance to use banisters, an attentiveness to the perils of debris across passages, and an avoidance of the wires and flexes that stretch across floors as well as the detached lights and swinging roof tiles that hang low. Floors might be less solid and bits of debris may be heavier than they appear. The moving body must perform in accordance with these contingencies and thus it is coerced into a more flamboyant, expressive, improvisatory passage through space at variance with the minor movements of a usually self-contained bodily comportment through the city, where a fixed stride, steady gait and minimal gestures delimit interaction with the environment. The body is thus enlivened by the varied operations it needs to perform in order to negotiate this obstacle course. Jolted out of its fixed composure, the body can rediscover unfamiliar exercises in which a more expansive physical engagement with surroundings is induced, a somatic experience bearing the memories of childhood play, a theme I develop in Chapter 5.

As illustrated by the range of recreational uses of ruins identified in the previous chapter, this liberated body is free to engage in pursuits that inscribe urban space as playground. Actions carried out for their pure kinaesthetic pleasure are enabled through the lack of any regulation and by the affordances of ruined structures. Crawling through dense undergrowth, scrambling over walls and under fences, leaping over hurdles and across gaps, kicking debris of various qualities

along the floor, throwing rubble at chosen targets and dancing and sprinting across stretches of flooring generate a rekindled awareness of the *jouissance* of gymnastic, expressive movement. Flights of fancy stimulated by mediated fantasies of the sort identified in the previous chapter can be enacted by clattering along rooftops or careering down decrepit fire escapes so that bodily endeavours are entwined with the stimulus of popular cultural imagery. This is no mere conjecture, for signs of playful exercise abound in ruins. Rope swings hang over wooden beams, windows are everywhere smashed and extemporised football pitches are created.

This disruptive pleasure is encapsulated in Borden's account of urban skateboarding which he describes as 'nothing less than a sensual, sensory, physical emotion and desire for one's own body in motion and engagement with the architectural and social other' (1998: 216). The performative display of technique and 'attitude' in skateboard parks and increasingly deserted urban areas, as well as pavements, roads, walls, stairs and benches, subverts the normative uses of the city. A heightened consciousness of the material textures of the city, and the sounds and tactile experiences they produce with the skater, as well as a transformed relationship of the body with verticality and diagonality, challenges the hegemony of normative linear, upright bodily positions, producing a more three-dimensional engagement with space. Skateboarding thus creates a body-centric

space produced dialectically with the built environment. Borden distinguishes skateboarding from the proliferating spectacles produced through commodification, including conscious intellectual and artistic performativity, as well as the narcissistic activities of shopping and body-building. Moreover, in contradistinction to the experiences delimited in these more seamless spaces, the ruin provides opportunities for the active engagement with the diverse affordances of space produced through dereliction and decay.

The sensual experience of a ruin is characterised by an immanent immersion in space rather than the mobilisation of a scopic, distanced sensing dominated by a gaze seduced by the symbolic and aesthetic placings of ornaments and images. While ruins are cluttered with visually fascinating scenes and can be densely read for signs of allegorical and symbolic significance, as I will discuss in Chapter 5, the sensual impact of ruined space can overwhelm a scopic approach. First of all, the tactilities of ruins are profoundly distinct from the smoothed over space of much city experience. As I will discuss in the following chapter, the tactilities engaged with as one moves across ruined space provoke sensations of matter crumbling underfoot, of the impact of the body on stray chunks of building material and broken glass, and an awareness of the feel of decaying matter as hands run across it. The opening of the ruin to the weather means that the body is apt to be buffeted by wind and rain, by gusts thick with dust, and atmospheres are often heavy with the presence of damp.

In a large, abandoned factory, the initial peculiarity of finding oneself alone in a vast space, devoid of other people and often stripped of fixtures, is compounded by the shroud of quiet which covers space and heightens awareness of sound. This relative quiescence contrasts with the dense soundscapes of other urban space, a hubbub composed of effusive machinery, blaring sounds and loud conversation. Yet as one becomes more habituated to the ruin, as it becomes more homely, other sounds emerge; for whilst the ruin insulates against the tumult of the outside world, a plethora of lower-decibel murmurs, soft echoes and scurries of unseen movement are enclosed to produce a more delicate soundscape. The removal of machinery and furniture means that noises echo: the drips of water, birdsong, eddies of winds, creaking machinery and doors, rustling of rodents, the cooing of pigeons and their flurries of urgent flight. The sound becomes fuller with the intrusions of weather from outside: an upsurge in clattering and squeaking during a gale, and throughout a shower of rain, a succession of drips of varying intensity produce a symphony of spatters and splashes which evoke the material upon which raindrops land – tin, foliage and stone. The stillness and the gentle noises that float through the ruin can evoke an absent soundscape – the whistling, shouts, talk and laughter, whirring machinery, singing and the radio which would have filled the air during its occupation – an evocation that provokes a tendency to stop and listen. Thus besides movement, the atmosphere and texture of the ruin can facilitate a disposition to become immersed in reverie, to slow down and stop, to opt out of the usual flow of city time. This quiescence is not a void but provides an occasion in which a pregnant silence can stimulate a slowing down that is promoted by the discernment of separate sounds rather than a dense fog of noise. Things sound different in the ruin. Echoes are rarely experienced in large spaces and one's own utterances are likely to be the only voice in a realm unpopulated by other humans.

Similarly, the deodorised smellscape of the contemporary city is rebuked by the rich brew of scents stewing in the ruin. Overwhelming is the mix of mustiness and decay, combining the mulch of stripped wallpaper, damp masonry, rotting wood and fungal colonies. Contrasting with the scent of mouldering are the aromas of flowers and grasses, particularly in spring and summer. But there are also remnants of the specific aromas that were involved in production, such as the caustic smell of lime, the acrid stench of chemicals and the overpowering stink of rubber. Smell, as has been noted by several commentators, is that sense which appears most able to provoke involuntary memories and forgotten sensations, and thus disrupts progress through space; but it is perhaps also that sense which is least developed in present times, and the strong smells which percolate through the ruin can be something of a shock for those solely accustomed to the city's commodified smells.

Being still in and moving through ruins foregrounds an awareness of our embodied relationship with space. Whilst I have emphasised that immersion in this broader sensual realm decentres the visual, this is not to suggest that the pleasures available to the eye – unconventional, uncodified pleasures – are pallid by comparison. Rather, habituation to common regimes of signification and aestheticisation is nonplussed by the innumerable meanings of sights in disordered space – by the interpretive possibilities available in the notices, artefacts, textures, fashions, forms of life and traces. A removal from assigned functions and placings means that what is beheld escapes from the dominant encodings of the city. Walking and looking in ruins is akin to the ways in which the Situationists showed how 'the dominant visual order of the city is unstable, liable to be shattered by the coming to light of repressed material and by ambiguities and eruptions in the ordering mechanisms associated with hegemonic ways of seeing' (Pinder, 2000: 378). Yet whilst there are plenty of things to gaze upon, a rather different experience of the visual evolves out of the ruinous sensual melange. As Latham puts it, 'this is a way of looking and experiencing the world in which the eye does not act to hold external objects in a firm contemplative gaze … it is a way of looking that feels its way round that place it finds rather than fixing that place with a distancing look … (it is) intensely tied up with the other sensations of the body …' (1999: 463). The eye thus moves across space but is generally not directed to carefully situated spectacles and signs, and visual experience is synaesthetic and affective. Although this book foregrounds the visual through photography, it is my hope that these images

will conjure up an imaginative apprehension of other sensations experienced in the ruin. For in the ruin, rather than the commodified sights and ordered spaces which, according to Fullagar (2001: 175), are entwined with dominant ways of looking at 'sanitised images of difference, picturesque nature and nostalgic emotion', the lack of visual distance allows affective, stimulating and ineffable sensations to emerge which foreground the self as body.

The somatic experience of the ruin might be compared to that of the 'body-without-organs' described by Deleuze and Guattari (1987), that escapes the grids of control which place and define its operations. This entity is an assemblage of affects within a field of immanence and desire, unhindered by disciplinary structures and orderly sense-making. This is also akin to what the same authors call 'becoming animal' (240), a state of being in which the bounds of identity temporarily dissolve and a sense of becoming is foregrounded by a physical, instinctual interaction with the world, where one prowls like a cat for instance, devoid of the self-awareness that usually accompanies forays into urban space.

In the ruin these sensations, productive of unnameable trajectories of desire, connect us to the otherness of place. Space here becomes replete with indeterminacy, immanent and ineffable feelings and countless conjectures and potentialities, which confound attempts to pin down spatial essence, to classify and categorise through representation and discourse. The space of the ruin thus generates the disruptive, affective and sensual intensities felt by the body which evade the 'cultural vocabularies' of 'theories of signification that are wedded to structure' (Massumi, 1996: 221).

Conclusion

This chapter has used the industrial ruin as a means to critique the over-regulated character of contemporary urban space. The ruin represents a space outside the Apollonian processes of disciplinary ordering, in which people are surveilled to ensure they enact 'appropriate' practices, conventions of performance which are also embodied in habitual behaviour. The sterile stages of the urban, commodified, single-purpose, aesthetically managed urban environments that disguise the excess of meaning and curtail the range of possible activities are in marked contrast to the ruin, barely framed as a functional space and replete with disorder. Whereas the factory was formerly stitched into an ordering network within which it assigned things, people and functions to specific realms and thus ensured the sustenance of spatial demarcations, the continual efforts required to uphold this order are now conspicuous by their absence.

Accordingly, the regulation of the urban everyday becomes manifest by its absence and by the possibilities made available in the ruin. Because ruins are difficult to bring into dominant systems of representation, because they can't be commodified without being entirely transformed, they contrast with the spectacles of the postmodern, themed city, and can stimulate imaginative, alternative practices which bring forth alternative and critical forms of consciousness. Fostering notions about how the world might be differently ordered in accordance with looser aesthetics, less managed spaces, bodies and things, and multi-interpretable signs, ruins can hint at potential futures in which individual creativities and desires are nurtured rather than being subsumed under individualistic consumption. Whilst initially disturbing, the disorder of a ruin possesses potentially progressive effects. For instance, as Richard Sennett (1994: 310) writes, the 'body comes to life when coping with difficulty', it is roused by the resistance which it experiences. Ruins are 'felicitous spaces', where the body may become released from self-policing but an awareness of corporeality is induced by the disruption of movement. Moments of confrontation, of self-displacement, are vital to preserve openness to stimuli, to awaken the senses. And the confrontation with the uncomfortable and the surprising can engender procedures of dialogue and negotiation which help to make sense of the jarring shocks of urban streets, and can encourage a critical approach to conventions. The acceptance of 'impurity, difficulty, and obstruction', according to Sennett, is 'part of the very experience of liberty' (309–10).

Finally, to underline some of these issues, I want to contrast visiting a ruin with dominant forms of tourism which are exemplary of the normative ways in which people interact with urban space. Tourism is typically organised around the capture of familiar, famous sights, undisturbed and seamless forms of mobility, the dissemination of digestible, pre-packaged information and reified discourses about places and cultures, a series of 'appropriate' activities centred upon consumption, and regularised itineraries which sew these sites together. Moreover, the space of tourism is increasingly themed, staged, aestheticised, disciplined, highly regulated, smooth, homogeneous and constituted through the interconnected sequence of similar spaces (see Edensor, 2005). Exploring ruins, on the other hand, cannot permit the smooth movement produced in tourism, for numerous obstacles present themselves and multiple routes may be followed. Movement is rough, disrupted and potentially perilous, replete with sensations other than the distanced gaze; no one is there to enforce performative norms, and indeed, there are no preparations for entry into, and performance upon, such a stage. There are no obvious spectacles around which to organise a tour, or which fit into expectations about what will be gazed upon, and sights will often be indecipherable. There is nothing to buy and nothing conforms to the staged aesthetics of tourist space. These experiences cannot be inserted into a pre-arranged vocabulary or classified as 'exotic' or 'typical'. I suggest therefore, that exploring a ruin is a kind of anti-tourism.

—4—

Materiality in the Ruin: Waste, Excess and Sensuality

In this chapter, I will explore how objects in ruins are ideally placed to rebuke the normative assignations of things, foregrounding questions about materiality, value and the apprehension of the material world. As I discussed in the previous chapter, the organisation of the social world depends upon the regular and predictable distribution of objects in space, artefacts which support habitual social performances and ways of living. These ubiquitous material arrangements can appear to present evidence of the common-sense obviousness of the ways in which the world is ordered, despite the huge cultural variations in the use, placement and circulation of objects across space and time. Usually unreflexively apprehended, they seem to be part of the way things are. By their physical presence and the ways in which they serve as fixtures around which habitual actions and routes are repetitively practised, objects consolidate a sense of being in place and provide proof of shared ways of living, of inhabiting space, of producing and sustaining values.

'A place for everything and everything in its place'. Such is the commonplace motto which underpins how objects are invariably subject to the social discipline inherent in the normative and habitual. Enmeshed in regimes of signification and common-sense ideas about usage and proper location, things are situated within a web of normative epistemological and practical associations, tethered to cultural uses and meanings. Marxists may point to this fixing as part of a wider process through which objects become fetishised, a process which masks the conditions of their production. Usefully, this reveals that the habitual and doxic understandings of things disguise other ways of conceiving them. However, it also restricts insight into the multifarious uses and interpretations to which objects may be subjected, for objects are always liable to transcend assigned meanings and purposes. They may be used in peculiar ways (as paperweights or garden ornaments), be given as humorous 'inappropriate' gifts, used in dissident rituals, curated in unusual ways on domestic shelves, or transformed through vernacular or artistic appropriation. Objects serve as media for communication between people through their semiotic meanings and the ways in which they are transacted (Dant, 1999). Possessing particular affordances and qualities, they are also able to stimulate sensual apprehension beyond the cognitive, and evoke memories and other thoughts that escape the pragmatism of an ordered social world.

I mentioned in the last chapter that social order persists through the maintenance of networks which variously comprise objects, humans, spaces, technologies and forms of knowledge, the meanings of the objects being assigned through their relations with other elements in these aggregations. One effect of this relationality is that 'political qualities and purposes become "fixed" in the material design and physical dimensions of technical artefacts themselves' (Pels, Hetherington and Vendenberghe, 2002: 7) as they are 'delegated intentionality and agency' (ibid.: 8). This rarely noticed material underpinning is necessary since 'social structures and symbolic representations are not solid enough to frame durable interactions and hold social reality in place' (ibid.), and an underlying material order is also required to sustain social order.

However, as the condition of objects in ruins makes most evident, these networks and their material ordering need to be constantly maintained to retain a regulated social order, for under modern conditions they are liable to disintegrate. And if not designed with a specific purpose in mind, things need to be subject to a 'containment' (Attfield, 2000), through which they are customised and domesticated to fit in with an existing spatial and material context. Unruly, initially uncategorisable things need to be assigned a place within existing material schema. Again this social-material order is exemplified in the factory, where machines are laid out in accordance with the imperatives of production: crates and bays hold finished or half finished manufactures, shelves accommodate tools, offices and their fixtures house paperwork, vehicles lie in garages, cupboards contain maintenance materials, and a host of receptacles, notices, utilities and equipment are similarly assigned to particular spaces and positions. Much labour and energy goes into the maintenance of these material systems of order, a regulated object world which the factory's denizens understand and come to inhabit unquestioningly, participating in the placing and replacing of things. Subsequently, however, once a factory is abandoned, under conditions of ruination, the previously obvious meaning and utility of objects becomes increasingly tenuous. Suddenly detached from a stabilising network which facilitated epistemological and practical security, the designated meanings and purposes of things evaporate. No-one now orders them and places them into specific categories, for their fate is placed within an uncertain situation which may be variously influenced by human and non-human animal users – a host of other life forms including plants, bacteria and fungi – the effects of the agency of other surrounding objects and structures, and bureaucratic and commercial decisions made elsewhere about the fate of the ruined site. And the possible destinies of things partly depend upon their material, sensual and functional

properties. Objects may be restored, curated or spirited away to serve the domestic purposes of plunderers, or they may be resituated to act as forms of shelter or comfortable fixtures for temporary human and other animal inhabitants. They may degenerate through processes of decay, may tumble to join other objects or mingle with other matter, or they may lie isolated on a large expanse of flooring. Whatever happens to them, however, radically removes them from their previous spatial contextualisation.

The sudden removal of the ordering contexts for objects in ruins highlights how things are always enmeshed within specific cultural contexts and embody particular histories. Objects have biographies by virtue of their emergence out of cultures expressive of particular aesthetics, functions and desires (Appadurai, 1986;

Kopytoff, 1986). These historical contexts and biographies can suddenly appear, are glaringly apparent as previously forgotten artefacts return to surprise us, evoking their era in their embodiment of an outdated style or function. And the curtailment of this historically confined fashion or process can starkly disclose that the biographies of objects in ruins have entered a critical phase, where the end of their story as identifiable, distinct and separate entities probably draws near. This awareness about the impending transformation of an object, or its conspicuous repositioning, can illuminate the inadequacy of dominant, cognitive, scopic ways of understanding and representing objects in space. In what follows, I will show how unruly objects in ruins can raise contemporary, critical questions about the nature of waste, and about the production of excessive matter and meaning. I will go on to look at the hybridity of matter and the transience of the artefact which masquerades as an enduring separate entity, and I will then discuss the sensual, affective, immanent encounter with the material world in ruins.

Wasted Spaces and Things

One way of considering ruins and their contents, as I have already discussed, is as waste. According to this notion, in the ruin all objects are equal, none assigned higher value than others, because they are all categorised as trash. They are useless and worn out, and therefore possess no value and can be, indeed ought to be, discarded. Since factories produce things for markets, objects situated in ruins also thereby escape another kind of classification in that they join the realm of waste products and are removed from the ranks of separate artefacts on shelves, in job lots, in typologies – according to function and price – that present themselves as commodities. The object's abrupt loss of the magic of the commodity – that it is a self-evident, separate thing of worth and value – seems to confirm Stallabrass's observation that 'commodities, despite all their tricks, are just stuff' (1996: 175).

The objects happened across in ruins are in some ways comparable to the artefacts which Walter Benjamin was attracted to in the fading arcades of pre-war Paris. Mingling with each other promiscuously, for Benjamin these evoked the desolation of the leftover commodity, now stranded from the recent, but seemingly far-distant past, discarded and outdated. Such was the speed of product innovation and the rapid changing of notions about what was deemed fashionable in that era, the no longer modish seemed suddenly archaic, surpassed by the latest new thing. Such objects drew attention to the unprecedented material destruction resulting from an advancing modern capitalism, which produced an accumulating pile of debris that relentlessly built up as manufacturers sought for ever-new technologies of production, and produced an endless stream of new items. In Benjamin's nightmarish vision, traces of the past are successively wiped out or consigned to a massive pile of the irrelevant, as part of a morbid cycle of 'repetition, novelty and death' (Buck-Morss, 1991: 97). Accordingly, waste materials offer evidence for a radical critique of the myth of universal progress driven by the supposedly innovative power of capitalism and technology. For by their presence they rudely display the evanescent character, the 'extreme temporal attenuation' (ibid.) whereby industrial techniques and commodities attain venerable status, and fashion produces instant obsolescence, so that the recent past becomes ancient history. Here we are faced with the converse of an ordering modernity in which the norm is for 'the denunciation of any form of fixity in favour of permanent flux' (Felski, 2000: 28). Abandoned objects in ruined factories equally evoke such rapid obsolescence although many of these artefacts, being unfinished, never attained the status of commodity and were never admitted to the circulation of things between factory, shop, home and disposal. In this sense, they can be conceived as victims of the devouring quest for the production of new commodities, entities whose becoming was curtailed through the sudden obsolescence of the things they were going to become. Though rapid in Benjamin's era, the processes of the rampant replacement of commodities and the resiting of production now operate on a far more global scale than when Benjamin was writing, indicating the even speedier production of obsolescence whereby whole urban areas and industries, together with their factories, their labour, the techniques and machinery used in production, and the objects they produced, all become waste.

In one sense, modern capitalism proceeds by forgetting the scale of devastation wreaked upon the physical and social world, for obliterating traces of this carnage fosters the myth of endless and seamless progress. However, lost and abandoned objects vividly convey this destruction. As previously celebrated and valuable commodities decay and become irrelevant in the continual creation of the new, they can be recognised as the dreams they always were, emblems of the fragility and destructiveness of unfettered capitalist production. The debris of successive industrial cultures, however, also reveals the fragility of a social order in which all that is solid turns to air. What now is classified as waste may once have signified progress, and indeed, in the products forged in these factories and in the shape of the buildings themselves lie clues to the fantasies of progress: 'the crumbling of the monuments that were built to signify the immortality of civilisation becomes proof, rather, of its transiency' (Buck-Morss, 1991: 170).

In the ruin, in confrontation with the scraps and shadowy forms of the recent past, the realisation dawns that the myth of an ever more advanced industrial production as emblematic of linear progress is instead better represented a circular process through which things become obsolete, are thrown away, later recycled or replaced in pursuit of the always new. Writing about the ruined dwellings, outbuildings and industrial sites of West Virginia, Stewart describes how in 'the discontinuity of these rough and fragmented places … the myth-of-history as progress breaks down and impacted objects reveal the cracks in its construction', because it 'embodies a continuous process of composition and decomposition' in which 'everything, including power itself, is constructed and transient' (1996: 96). She goes on to show how these 'luminous fragments of things in decay' both 'mimetically demonstrate a partially excluded but re-membered real' and the inevitability of this passing, for 'wrecked material becomes a sign, at once, of the power of history on a place and of the transitoriness of history itself' (Stewart, 1996: 95).

The sudden reappearance of things from the past, things that emerge from the ineluctable, dispassionate consignment of things into history, can shock us into the realisation that there was a sudden passing which we never properly acknowledged and, more than this, that these disappearing things were objects we might have regarded fondly, as part of our own histories. Thus we might stumble across the seemingly archaic décor of wallpaper and colour scheme, the apparent hideosity of the furniture lying in vacant offices, posters of yesterday's footballers and pop stars, toys and mascots from popular culture used ironically as kitsch props by workers, the motifs of calendars and even print styles, shelves, phones and a host of other fixtures which embody the outmoded, the styles and fashions represented in old catalogues and the objects themselves lying in storage spaces – tiles, car seats, pottery and metal furniture. At one level, such objects appear part of 'an

accelerated archaeology' (Stallabrass, 1996: 176) whereby they suddenly seem absurd or comical, out of time as well as out of place. Yet these articles can result in surprising jolts of recognition that bring back knowledge and tastes that were thought to have been consigned to the past, forgotten forever. In this sense then, these objects convey something of our own pasts as well, for they are part of the clutter which we too have left behind, perhaps because the impulses to 'progress' and move on emerge out of our own modern desires to manage ourselves. We are thus complicit with this wasting.

A sense about the optimistic promise for the future which industrial production signified, and the global power it conveyed, is especially salient in a postcolonial Britain, where the factory and its products – sold far and wide – symbolised 'the workshop of the world'. Now this workshop has been largely dismembered, its products manufactured elsewhere and its labour laid off. The connective tissue between most locations of industrial production across the UK is that imperial project, where materials were imported, things fashioned and finished goods sent out to colonial markets. The rosy-hued expectations about future power as well as the fears about imperial dissolution are thus evoked by the demise of Britain's old industrial base, still present in ruins and the wasted manufactures they contain. Particularly evocative of this vanished network of imperial power are those discarded products stamped with the label 'Made in Britain'. Equally, many of the manufactures which have accumulated in ruined factories carry the marks of their places of production, signifiers of a local industrial prowess and tradition embodied in these objects. This increasingly ghostly geography of the heavy industrial past is replaced, as the 'new realities' of global competition manifest by the less concrete products of the information and service industries replace earlier manufacturing power and fold these and other places into the economy in different ways.

A focus on these past dreams about the future might seem inescapably morbid but Benjamin insisted that this was not so, that rather than conceiving of this cycle of disillusion as a hopeless symbol of inevitable death and decay – much like the Victorian writers cited in the first chapter imagined ruins to prefigure the demise of empire, 'man's' work and the hapless fantasies of human pride and the longing for posterity – things were not so bleak. For such material emblems of capitalist modernity could be recouped as useful examples that clearly revealed capitalism's inevitable limitations and weaknesses and fortified socialist arguments about the necessity for more progressive forms of social organisation: 'the debris of industrial culture teaches us not the necessity of submitting to historical catastrophe, but the fragility of the social order that tells us that this catastrophe was necessary' (Buck-Morss, 1991: 170).

Besides conceiving them as exemplary manifestations of the endless waste produced by capitalism, Benjamin also searched for congealed life in discarded things, seeking out their allegorical potentialities. The commodity, as well as other objects, appears as an entity which possesses a fixed meaning and use-value, and when these are exhausted or irrelevant, the subsequent loss of its exchange value turns it into waste. Yet this process hides a multitude of other dimensions not least, the effort that went into the design and manufacture of the object, as well as its availability to semiotic interpretation, its materiality, and its aesthetic and sensual capacities. Such histories and qualities suggest a quite different set of inferences and ideals. For instance, Benjamin wished to 'engender the rediscovery and release of the utopian traces which lay dormant within material objects, blasting away the fetishism and reifications that were embedded within them' (Latham, 1999: 456). Like the articles Benjamin stumbled upon, the apparent waste that clutters ruined space can be used to recoup ideas and activities that surrounded its production. The mental and physical energies that have gone into the production of objects, and the team work necessary to keep the production process ticking along, point to the potential available in human endeavour, in its inventiveness and skill, and in the latent possibilities of collective work. In addition, bereft of their commodified, packaged forms, devoid of sheen, the form, texture and tactility, the aesthetic qualities of objects, can be appreciated anew, without the trappings of display. In another twist, the apparent out-of-placeness of discarded objects can appear peculiar, but as Stallabrass remarks, although the 'meaning of trash would seem to lie in a surreal absurdity ... by taking it seriously, this very quality may come to illuminate the real absurdity of the situation in which it is produced' (1996: 173), and question the necessity of producing such objects in the first place. This reveals that one of the characteristics of power is the ability to make decisions about what is required, and therefore what objects get to be produced and in what form. It therefore also becomes clear that one of the lineaments of power is the authority to make waste, to decide what is no longer of use and disseminate common-sense ideas about what ought to be over and done with. For speculators and planners, the detritus of the past hinders a view of land as potentially available for redevelopment, obscures the possibility that wasteland might be turned into abstract space in the quest for new profits (Lefebvre, 1991). Yet the other side of the decommissioning of space and things is their reclamation by industries concerned with renovation, recycling and preservation and by less organised individuals and groups.

Thus objects may pass through the process of becoming waste but then be refigured as valuable, whether through being worked upon to refashion or renovate them to their assumed original appearance, or by being recategorised as 'antique' or 'found sculpture'. As Appadurai (1986) has shown, obsolescence can be a

somewhat fluid category, for whilst objects are designated their roles, these can be far from static and may pass through a range of assignations, from the commodity, to treasured keepsake, to the worn out and discarded. Cherished things may become unwanted baggage that must be expelled as a symbolic entity through the desire for a 'fresh start', or there may be great unwillingness to let go of a familiar object-companion (Lucas, 2002). Alternatively, as Thompson (1979) has argued in his tripartite schema, objects may be conceptualised as 'transient' – possessing a a finite use-value which depreciates over time – or as 'durable', where conversely, value remains the same or accrues over time. Distinguished from these objects are those with 'zero value', that which is assigned as 'rubbish'. This latter category, according to Thompson, serves to mediate the fall or rise in value of the other two forms, in that transient objects need to become rubbish before they can become durable. These social assignations are mediated via the power wielded by 'experts' such as antique and art dealers, and a distinction-seeking elite, who constantly attempt to maintain the value of that which they identify and own as 'exquisite' and 'exceptional'.

Although useful in identifying the mobilities of value of things and the dynamic social processes through which the value of objects change, Thompson's rather universalising conception of rubbish appears to ignore other processes through which objects lose and become re-enchanted with value. The idea that transient objects must succumb to waste status is surely not an immutable law, for the

transient can be catapulted into durability through reassignation. Similarly, the durable may become instantaneously value-less due to sudden transformations in politics, fashion or scholarly evaluation (see Moser, 2002). Thompson also neglects the numerous contextual possibilities through which objects may be assigned value for nostalgic or affective reasons, through dissident cultural practice – such as punk stylistics which reclaims rubbish as of symbolic value – or in terms of the spatial context within which an object is situated. Thus, situated in ruins, the work table may accrue value by virtue of it having been used in a particular context, by the fact that the marks of toil etched onto its surface give it a pleasing and meaningful patina which testifies to its use. Similarly, the found sculptural object might only be recognised as possessing an aesthetic charge due to its chance positioning, its recontextualisation. Moreover, the degree to which things are recycled varies enormously. For instance, the ruined spaces and rubbish heaps of the developing world provide important economic resources in conditions of subsistence, so that obsolete commodities, or bits of them, can be taken and reassembled, utilised in the production of household necessities and ingeniously fabricated saleable goods.

At a more institutional level however, as O'Brien (1999) points out, rubbish is central to industrial societies. The waste disposal industry must plan how to dispose of and manage five billion tonnes of rubbish per decade in UK. Accordingly, waste technologies are mobilised to deal with the surfeit of stuff, with rubbish being sifted into various categories which can be recycled, graded according to its suitability as fertiliser, or made safe and turned into landfill. Indeed, the British 1995 Environment Act identifies sixreen different kinds of waste (Lucas, 2002: 8). Through these technologies then, use-value may have drained out of objects, but they are then converted into different matter which can become sources of lucrative exchange value, highlighting the contradictory discourses which surround waste, simultaneously declaring it to be void of value and valuable. Even where rubbish is consigned to rubbish heaps and landfills, it may be subject to archaeological exploration or the use of metal detectors – and formerly discarded rubbish can be found to be newly valuable (O'Brien, 1999: 267). This reveals that in many cases 'rubbish is temporally, socially, politically and economically dynamic' (ibid.: 271) and is contested, so that what may be construed as ugly or obstructive may be recouped as beautiful and accorded commodity status. This dynamic cycle, where the over-and-done with comes back to life, highlights how the consignment of things to the dump, or the assignment of the appellation 'waste' to space, is an effect of a cycle which can be 'understood as an interconnected series of processes ... of wasting, reappropriation, and consumption of urban matter and space' (Neilsen, 2002: 56). And yet more broadly, we might consider this social cycle to be superimposed upon a larger cycle, part of a wider ecology through which all matter is continually subject to decomposition and recomposition, reshaped and denuded by flows of energy and tides of change: a natural cycle revealed by the rapid transformation of matter in ruins, which is always predominant in the final analysis.

The speedy erasure of waste and the urgency with which the materials of the past are consigned to history are required to sustain an economy which endlessly produces the newly fashionable. And yet despite the efforts to erase waste from the landscape, it is apt to return – whether as seepage of chemicals into water supplies, as the marine detritus which covers a beach or as landfill exposed in a storm. The massive production of waste through the torrent of discarded packaging, obsolescent technologies and outmoded fashions means that its obliteration is always partial. Such is the case with those ruins where efficient means for their demolition and the disposal of their constituent matter have not been mobilised. Although ruins have been assigned as useless space, the objects within them have a more ambiguous status, for whilst they occur in that space they have not been specifically sorted and classified into piles ready for dumping, and thus possess an intermediate quality which renders them ripe for reappropriation. They are excess matter which has not been disposed and therefore not consigned to fixity through annulment. Ruins contain excess, waste with which people can construct meaning, stories and practices, objects which possess 'unforseen value and status insofar as they lack contour … precisely because they are fluid as well as opaque and resistant to fixity'(Neville and Villeneuve, 2002: 5).

Material Excess and the Recontextualisation of Objects

In this section I look at the material excess that is produced through ruination, the impact of decay upon objects, their tendency to become indistinct and hybridised things, and the aesthetic effects of objects situated in ruins.

The production of waste and its attempted erasure is part of a speeded-up, modern condition through which there is an increasingly intensive regulation of materiality. Whilst 'expelling and discarding is more than biological necessity – it is fundamental to the ordering of the self' (Hawkins and Muecke, 2003: xiii), modern regimes of disposal have developed systematic modes of dealing with unwanted matter. Subterranean networks take away sewage, rubbish is conveyed to increasingly sectioned-off reprocessing sites, and even gas, electricity and water – the substances that keep modern cities and industries operating – are conveyed and channelled underground. This testifies to the role of hygienist ideologies in keeping material associated with pollution, disease and contagion away as a means to maintain spatial purity. Waste is dirty and disorderly, is unseemly matter out of place as it spills into ordered space, coming into contact with other, apparently discrete objects, and it must be expelled from this sphere, consigned to an other confined and bounded space where it may freely mingle with similarly discarded, dirty waste (Douglas, 1966).

In the ruined factory, however, the vigilant clearance of matter has become redundant and so we confront an effusion of material, strewn across surfaces and protruding from all angles. The changing configuration of this mingling glut of stuff is dependent on the rate of decay. Because materials are usually ordered and situated according to regimes of ordering space and things, the appearance of an apparently chaotic blend can affront sensibilities more used to things in their place. Although the fate of nearly all things is to eventually become waste when they lose their value or relevance, they tend to be swept out of view, in giant heaps of rubbish or as composite elements of landfill. Here, the production of excess material is all too clear, and yet it provides a space which can be scavenged for useful pickings, like the municipal rubbish tips which are now largely secured against public intrusion.

Ruination produces a defamilarised landscape in which the formerly hidden emerges; the tricks that make a building a coherent ensemble are revealed, exposing the magic of construction. The internal organs, pipes, veins, wiring and tubes – the guts of a building – spill out, as informal and official asset-strippers remove key materials such as tiles and lead. The key points of tension become visible, and the skeleton – the infrastructure on which all else hangs – the pillars, keystones, support walls and beams stand while less sturdy material – the clothing

THIS WALL IS NOW AVAILABLE IN PAPERBACK!

or flesh of the building – peels off. And the hidden networks are laid open, released from their confinement behind walls and under floors. The sewers, tram lines, pulley systems, water pipes, drainage channels and ventilation shafts appear, and phone lines and electric wires break out from their imprisonment, often in seemingly exuberant display. The conduits through which matter and energy flowed, those channels which connected the factory to the outside, which took away its waste and brought in its power become severed from wider networks or gummed up with extraneous matter like clogged arteries.

This coagulating debris emanates from the building itself and reveals how the sheer profusion and diversity of matter which is used to construct a building tends to be disguised by its form. Formerly contained within specific places, densely packed within solid agglomerations of matter, subject to painting or other aesthetic schemes which conceal the presence of diverse material quantity, a compilation of varied materials through which the building has been organised bursts out of assigned positions in an efflorescence of deconstruction. Catalysed by contact with moisture, temperatures and non-human life, the latent energies of matter emerge and act to transform their containment in the form of a building, producing a ruin.

Tiles cascade onto the floors of ruins and slide down roofs, gathering in piles at the base of outer walls. Mortar is released from its binding function, escaping in fragile slivers, and bricks crumble, attacked by living things, and congregate in piles. Plaster disintegrates and violates the formerly smooth surfaces of walls revealing fracturing lath; hardboard and plywood peel apart and concrete fractures, exposing rusting reinforced steel. In offices, wallpaper shears off walls in great strips. Polystyrene tiles, vinyl and other coverings hang down from ceilings filling up the upper dimensions of rooms, space that is usually uncluttered by matter. The metal fixtures of the factory, the steel tables and machinery, progressively rust as the building opens itself to the elements. Paint peels in extravagant patterns, blistering and cracking, and following the attention of 'vandals' the jagged edges of fractured windows frame outside scenes whilst shards of glass cover floors, adding to the profusion of animal, vegetable and mineral substances. Floors are strewn with clinker, plastic, piles of thick lime, cleaning agents, adhesives, grease, oil, pitch. Furniture stands bereft. Cogs and machine bits, screws, springs, wheels and axles are marshalled into clusters by the action of wind and water. Whether through rain or the effects of burst water pipes, large pools of water may accumulate in pits and hollows, constituting a broth filled with fragments or the shimmering hues of chemicals spilt from their containers. Receptacles of all sorts – packages, cupboards, barrels, crates, palettes and buckets – erode and discharge their contents whilst capturing other matter as it falls and flows unpoliced along floors and down walls. Slit-open sacks spill their contents across floors.

Besides the unfinished, stacked products that linger in storage areas, ruins also host another kind of material which eludes classification, namely the residues, off-cuts and by-products that emerge from the production process and litter shop floors. In their peculiar unfamiliarity, these articles escape easy identification and provide more material for speculative interpretation. These metal spirals, shearings, plastic mouldings, filings, blobs and other forms of scurf are another kind of material excess that mix with those more evidently discrete objects and from which they gradually become indistinguishable. More obviously identifiable are the reams of overflowing paperwork across ruined space, covering tables and floors. These chits, bills, adverts, posters, orders, labels, notices, signs, letters, stencils are eaten by mice and slowly transform into a pile of indistinguishable pulp. Personal artefacts of the workforce such as clothes, boots, mugs, hardhats and gloves add to the jumble.

What may initially present itself as a large collection of separate, intermingling artefacts, gradually becomes a mass of stuff in which it increasingly becomes difficult to determine the discreteness of things. But the divergencies of decomposition also highlight the qualities of matter and their resistance or susceptibility to the agents of decay. The protection afforded to outside wood through paint or creosote can only hold out for so long, most stones are vulnerable to crumbling once damp saturates mortar and the fixing together of matter in building assembly is

undone by the ceaseless searching for signs of weakness by opportunistic tendrils and roots. Water will eventually seep through cracks and render all materials in a ruin susceptible to attack; then things will erode according to their solubility, and this process is affected and often exacerbated by the chemical compounds which are dissolved in the water: chemicals picked up as water trickles through the ruin or present in acid rain. With the opening up of roofs and windows, unadulterated light pours into derelict buildings, causing paint and varnish to blister and peel. And a susceptibility to attack by bacteria, algae and fungi similarly depends upon the location of objects and their chemical constituency. Fungi and moss exploit the smallest cracks in stones and tiles – especially stones like sandstone and limestone – to send down minute threads that penetrate deep and start their destructive work, laying the groundwork for other plants to exploit growing fissures. Likewise the local climate, and plant and animal ecology, are context-specific factors that shape how buildings decay. The presence of humidity and damp produce faster decay whereas water in a cold climate releases the power of freeze-thaw action to crack structures apart. Similarly, certain insects are more destructive and certain trees more adaptable and exploitative of built structures than others.

Objects in ruins are stripped down in stages so that initial signs of decay, a mild tarnish or rust, signify future eventualities: that period where an object retains its shape but has become hollowed out or has lost its density; the time when it starts to shed parts of its body and then starts to fragment, surrounded by small particles of its former self; and finally, where it becomes a pile of dust or rubble, becoming indistinguishable as separate object. Each of these phases stimulates different con-jectures and sensations but all dispel the magic of the commodity as a separate and unique entity worthy of ownership. For unruly and abandoned objects enmeshed within processes of degeneration are dispossessed of that use or exchange value with which they were formerly attributed, lost to the world of things that perform

useful work, signify status and decorate space. Like the artefacts assembled by artist Joseph Beuys, the ruin is a space akin to 'a playroom or the cemetery for lost objects which never made it to the world of categories' (Taussig, 2003: 17).

Processes of decay also serve to differentiate between formerly homogeneous items, so that a neatly aligned wall of bricks, or a row of paving slabs are attacked by the contingencies of agents and exploited in accordance with the minute distinctions which inheres in each, formerly similar object. Each brick, tile, beam or slab develops its own particularity, is covered in its own colourful patterns created by lichen and moss, crumbles differently and takes an idiosyncratic irregular shape. The consignment of things to categories and functions through which they are assembled together, in ranks, is thus defeated by their gradual dispersal and emergent individuality, a reconstitution which impacts upon the beholder for, as Dekkers remarks, as 'different shapes appear, different feelings are evoked than the ones we felt before' (1997: 29).

But paradoxically, besides the emergent individualism of things in the process of ruination, they also become inseparable from other things in peculiar compounds of matter. Within this material excess, things get wrapped around each other, they penetrate each other, they merge to form weird mixtures. Thus objects progressively become something else, or become hybrids. The natural intrusions mentioned in Chapter 2 inveigle their way into the fabric of the factory. Ferns and flowers spring out of cracks and saplings emerge later, buckling concrete and plaster as their roots disaggregate wholeness. Fungus grows on wood, wallpaper and upholstery, at first producing encrustations, discolouring and ornamentation but it ultimately melds with its host and disaggregates it. Moss accumulates on brick. All kinds of fabric delicately crumbles, thins out and gaps appear. Material gets gnawed by mammals and insects, or is worked upon by bacteria, often producing elaborate patterns of warping, peeling and mouldering, adding squiggles, blotches, mosaics and splashes of colour. Bird shit, rust and dust coat machines. Streaks of rain mixed with dirt are splayed on walls, geometric shards of sunlight bisect floors and walls. Ferns and lichens prosper in areas of damp, nests colonise corners and ledges, spilling their building materials, corners are filled with thick layers of cobweb laden with the crunchy remnants of captured prey. The entropic tendency for material to merge, through its disordering and disaggregation, ends in a thick layer of mulch, a decayed mass which is not finished with but may be colonised by new forms of life and usage.

This hybridisation undoes the order of things, transgressing the assigned boundaries between things, and between objects and nature. As things decay they lose their assigned status as separate objects. Deteriorating material separates into parts due to gravity or the tendency of weakening joints to stretch away from each other. Things give up their solidity, their form, yielding to the processes which reveal them as aggregations of matter, erasing their objective boundaries, those edges which could be felt and looked at and suggested that the object was inviolable as a discrete entity. The barrier between one thing and another evaporates as they merge to form indistinguishable matter or a separate hybrid artefact. Piles of things cling together and merge to form a solid mass, the boundaries between things – which are after all, a mass of separate molecules forged into specific forms – disappear. This exposes how the physical deconstruction of objects, which have been inserted into a material world structured to withstand ambiguity through the discrete positioning of things, reveals the artifice of these designations. At this remove from the ordered world of objects in space, and contextualised within spaces of clutter and dirt, things 'comment ironically on themselves' (Stallabrass, 1996: 174).

Accidental sculptural forms emerge from the violence of collapse and the effects of hybridisation. Twisted metal, a bank of shattered windows, a trail of differently coloured paperwork, a container spilling its contents, a fallen beam, an isolated machine, stacks of ageing boxes and a multitude of unidentifiable objects lie inscrutably across floors. In individual isolation such forms possess a presence, a weight asserted through their reconfigured form. Previous function is a faint echo. Positioned in a new location or adopting a different stance, where they previously possessed an evident purpose, objects are made unfamiliar, and those enigmatic things whose function can only be guessed at add to the bewildering spatial redistribution of material forms. Leaning askew, tilting towards each other, squashed into confined spaces or violated into contorted patterns, things in ruins contravene our usual sense of perspective; they rebuke the way things are supposed to assume a position in regimented linearity or are separated from each other at appropriate distances. Reframed within spaces that have been reconfigured – through the removal of certain fixtures, the erasure of boundaries between inside and outside, and the demolition of doors, walls and other dividing barriers – objects are more overtly positioned in a sort of queer gallery of the neglected and the inscrutable.

Inside ruins, objects, textures and fragments fall out of their previously assigned contexts to recombine like elements in dreams, a random re-ordering which is determined by where things land or are thrown. Elements composed of many sorts of material mingle in array: masonry crumbles, ceilings fall down and wild arrangements of heterogeneous materials are organised into expressive forms, comprising chaotic and unusual juxtapositions where forms of matter usually kept apart meld or stand together in peculiar pairs. As Yaeger remarks, in that which is assigned as trash 'everything mutates; we see the transformation of oblivion where what has been forgotten mingles with other forms, producing strange new products, changed compounds' (2003: 112).

Things become detached from their use, their class and category as they stand in odd assemblage or in isolation. Yet standing in curious relationships with each

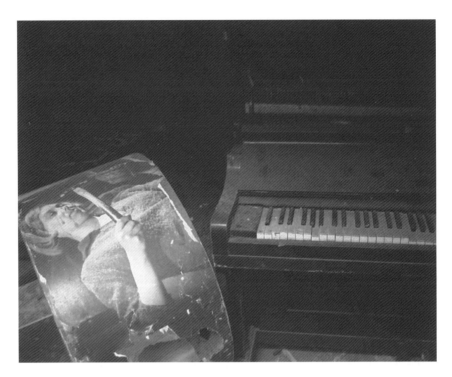

other, their conjoining suggests that they are related and communicate in unfathomable ways. Again, this aesthetic is partly shaped around the blurring of boundaries between objects usually kept apart, and barriers which determine where things should be placed – between the sensible and the senseless, the rural and the urban, the inside and the outside and the past and the present – become defunct. Such unfamiliar amalgamations provoke conjectures about how they came to be positioned thus, conjure up uncanny and bizarre scenarios, fantastic happenings through which monstrous forces have inverted the order of things. It can be difficult to figure out how and why certain objects have arrived at their current destination, for they may appear too big to move without lifting machinery, or are seemingly not the sorts of artefacts that ought to be situated there. Such location is a matter for speculation. Perhaps such objects testify to other people passing through ruined space, playing with things or cobbling together forms of vernacular art on the hoof. Alternatively, such objects may have been situated through non-human agency, through the collapse of flooring or by the action of animals.

Objects in ruined factories, bent out of shape, decaying and cast adrift from their assigned settings often appear as sensuous and peculiar sculptures, taking on a curious, appealing resonance by virtue of their chance recontextualisation in space. In the previous chapter I discussed the ways in which the ordering of space, activities and objects secures social and industrial order. In the ruin, things become

liberated from the surrounds which secure their purpose and meaning: their form suddenly becomes foregrounded, whether they lie amidst a sea of wreckage or stand isolated in large areas of flooring. Formerly appraised for their utility in the production process but now devoid of it, their uncanny beauty calls for an appreciation of their previously disregarded material and formal qualities. One effect of this aesthetic recharging can be the conjuring up of a sort of mundane surrealism where the reasons for their presence, their relationship to space and other objects, and their biographies conjure up dream-like and fantastical imaginings that interrogate the regulations of the normative object world. And yet the surreal is that which has been conjured by humans to appear out of place, whereas in ruins there is a supra-human agency which leads to the capricious re-siting of things.

In the same way, objects in ruins are rarely charged with the ornamental, the decorative, the functional or the kitsch. For instance, appraisal of an object as 'kitsch' depends upon it being recontextualised, so that its mooted aesthetic value is subject to contestation. This requires that the object be sited in a further context – on a shelf where it stands out in contrast to other, more 'tasteful' artefacts or as part of an array of objects classified as 'kitsch' – so that it is recognised as 'kitsch'. In the ruin, the barriers between the valued and valueless dissolve and so it is difficult to designate objects as kitsch.

In addition to the peculiar objects which populate ruins, also mysterious are those objects which are no longer there but announce their absent presence by the hole or shape or silhouette they leave behind: the tracing out of a stairway against a wall, a rectangular patch of brighter paint or wallpaper which announces the removal of a cupboard, the indentations in the wall left by shelving. Besides the aesthetic effect left by the imprint of the absent object, further conjecture is stimulated about how and why such an object has been removed and whether it now nestles in another context.

The spatial redistribution of objects in the ruin also draws attention to the qualities which inhere in their materiality, the stuff of which they are made, as I will shortly discuss. These processes, through which things have been manufactured by the melding together of specific materials, invoke the sensuous labour of those made them, assembled them, forged their shape and smoothed away the rough edges to produce the finished article. Yet in an increasingly post-industrial world, in which most people have become detached from any knowledge of the relatively recent skills used in manufacturing industry, objects used in the production processes – the machines, fixtures and tools – are entirely unfathomable. Formerly in the province of specialised knowledge and practical expertise, they have been abandoned by those who knew how to utilise them, and as objects employed in possibly obsolete techniques of manufacture, have been surpassed by new objects stitched into systems of technical expertise elsewhere. Yet these machines and tools imply the bodies of those who made things habitually; they adapted and fashioned their labouring bodies in the pursuit of familiar tasks, and incorporated tools into their bodily practices, thus constituting the human-object hybrids which make things. The fixtures and fittings, the work benches, the furniture in rest areas that remain in ruins all summon up the people who became accommodated to their material presence as part of the second nature of factory inhabitation. Again, such objects offer their enigmatic presence as a subject for conjecture and invite us to imagine the feeling of working in and inhabiting the material world of the factory.

The Affordance of Ruined Things

The excess of matter in ruins and the surplus energies within the objects chanced upon are not merely open to aesthetic and semiotic reappraisal, but impact upon the body as they move through ruined space: 'waste can touch the most visceral registers of the self – it can trigger responses and affects that remind us of the body's intensities and multiplicities' (Hawkins and Muecke, 2003: xiv). All those things 'that surprise, that disturb, that introduce unpredictability' (ibid.) are not merely mentally apprehended but sensually experienced.

I have discussed the sensual ways of moving through ruined space and this is complemented by the sensual engagement with ruined matter, where encountering unfamiliar industrial objects such as furniture and machinery can foreground an awareness of the materiality of things: the slabby thickness of a steel door or the pock-marked, splintery texture of a wooden work bench, the well-worn smooth-ness of a wooden stairway's handrail, the mouldering dampness of paper and wall-paper, the crumbly plaster on the walls, the icy presence of iron machinery, the weight of an empty oil drum, the jagged remnants of manufactures, the oily surface of a series of cogs, the encrusted exteriors of foundry fittings, the pliability of wires and thin metal strips, the brittleness of rotting matter, the cushioned con-sistency of moss and the sliminess of wet, rotting wood. Such things are exciting to the touch, seem to encourage the hand to run over them and explore their con-sistency. In a non-exhibitionary space replete with artefacts that have not been placed with a selling or an educative function in mind, the feel of the substance of the thing invites the body to sense this material otherness. Things are available to pick up, to stroke and throw, to lift and pull apart.

Producing objects usually entails the shearing off of rough edges and textures, but the process of decay and assault by other objects, humans and forms of life produces roughness once more, erases smoothness and sheen. The ruin is no longer a space in which velvety textures, polished surfaces, colour coded design, even hue, plush carpeting, noiseless machinery and an absence of clutter prevail.

The falling apart of things and the invasion of other external matter, besides confounding the normative aesthetic appraisal of objects, reveals hidden tactilities. In the previous chapter, I discussed the ordering of the senses in contemporary urban settings through the minimisation of unsettling sounds, smells, textures and sights. In ruins this policing of the sensualities of space to reduce or commodify smells, sounds and textures does not intrude on the effusion of the provocative affordances of things. This initially startling confrontation with the evocative matter of objects reminds us that things are never merely semiotic entities swirling through a hyperreal sign-system, but are made out of specific materials, have a weight and a texture. This reacquaintance with the materiality of things that were yet to be fashioned or had already been wrought into recognisably half-finished or finished products recalls the sensuous, embodied knowledge of these substances possessed by the workers who inhabited these now ruined spaces. The creation of things out of formless quantities of matter bespeaks the acquisition of the of workers' habitual ability to process, mould and assemble bits and pieces, requiring an awareness about the qualities of stuff which emerge from the routine engagement with its materiality. This awareness of materiality also remembers the ways in which all manufactures are composed and assembled out of 'raw' material, that they have been forged through skills which shape form and texture, and that they are, in some sense, reverting to an original material indistinctiveness which preceded their extraction, cropping and stacking.

In the ruin the energies of matter are catalysed by the agencies of cold and damp, or by creatures which thrive in very different conditions from those in which objects were previously housed. By bursting free of their form, those energies are sensually imparted by the sheer presence of objects and matter, which become endowed with a material charisma. As you wander through ruins, you come across and may avoid or step into glutinous pools of grease, the caustic acidity of certain chemicals may assault the nose, the face may suddenly become enveloped in a thick veil of cobwebs. The shards of glass that have been the target of pleasurable destruction litter the floor, making a soundless walk through ruined space impossible. The walking body is thus unable to insulate itself against these material intrusions. The sweeping of pavements and the efforts of individuals and cleaning industries to maintain smoothness and minimise the mess of stuff are absent here, and so matter impinges upon, is inhaled and absorbed and expelled by the body, whose outer surfaces become coated with filth and grime: the residues of formerly solid matter cover skin, hair and clothes. Walking through an old engineering workshop, my boots became progressively caked with the thick grease, mingled with ground plaster, bird shit and other detritus that coated the entire floor. Such was the viscous tackiness of this gunge as it adhered to the soles of my boots that my height was raised three inches, producing an unfamiliar gait and visual perspective.

Dust – the enemy of modern regimes to banish dirt, to clean and order by water, light, vacuum cleaners and chemical cleansers – lies thick in ruins (see Amato, 2000). Here, the endless quest to banish stuff classified as dirt has temporarily ceased and the experience of the filthy returns as hands, clothes and face are coated and clogged with dust and grime. And dust is composed out of a multitude of materials, is a compound mix of innumerable elements. Whilst this collection of particles of matter may be specific to the industry of the location, so that it is primarily constituted by soot, grime and other miniscule forms of detritus produced by industrial processes, it is also likely to contain the residues of animals and plants (decayed organic matter, seeds, droppings), the crumbling infrastructure of stone, brick, wood, plaster and rust, and also, in small part, the shed skin and hair of the thousands of workers of the factory, crumbs from their snacks and threads from their clothing. And so walking through the ruined factory entails the breathing in of a rich compound which may be resisted by evasive action in the face of material attack: the handkerchief to the face, the blocking of the nostrils and the shielding of the arm from unexpected rays of sun breaking through fractured roofs. However, a defence against dirt may be accompanied by a sense of alterity which evokes what it feels like to be dirty in an age in which there is a cosmetic onslaught upon dirt, or it may evoke memories of grubbiness in childhood or conjure up the layered, caked muckiness of the labouring body in the factory.

The agency of decaying and otherwise transformed matter means that it might creak when walked upon or crumble to the touch, might give off fragments which attach themselves to the body. The facility of unpoliced objects and matter to impress the body with their changing qualities under conditions of decay and deterioration, with their hardness, dampness, slipperiness, roughness and coldness, is the evocation of a materiality which has been liberated. In ruins, freed from the necessity to disguise its nature in the service of commodification, or escaped from the realms to which it was consigned, no longer swept up or polished away, the materiality of matter returns. Materiality then, like the ghostly intrusions of the previous denizens of the factory (to be discussed in the next chapter) and the reverberations of ruined space, invades the porous body, a body not bounded but open to the impacts of stuff. Such porosity speaks of the 'ability of strange substances to cross the subject's own boundaries' where the body is a 'threshold or passage', characterised by 'multiple surfaces open to other surfaces' (Fullagar, 2001: 179).

Conclusion

In this chapter, I have shown that the experience of materiality in the industrial ruin has the potential to alter the normative apprehension of objects. To start with, I have looked at how such things help us to question the conventions and politics through which activities, places and things are assigned as waste. I then explored the material excess evident in ruins, leading on to a discussion about the aesthetics of the varied, multiple objects encountered, the mystery which surrounds their location and function by virtue of their unusual situations, the juxtapositions which occur between things, and the hybridities which evolve, merging objects with life-forms and other objects. These processes act to blur boundaries between things and highlight the illusion of discrete permanence which is attached to objects and places. Following this, I discussed how the sensual effects of objects in ruins, often under conditions of decay, produces textures, smells and tactilities which provoke a sensual experience of things rarely beheld in the modern city.

Objects are other to humans, although they are usually imbricated in sensual, cognitive and practical engagements with the social which delimits the scope for using, interpreting and sensing them. Things in ruins, however, are charged with a more radical alterity. Lacking any obvious meaning, feeling different, unclear in their function, aesthetically indecipherable and out of place, these artefacts pose an alternative way of relating to objects that goes beyond buying and possessing them, domestically displaying and enfolding them, and using them as common-sense fixtures around which everyday life is organised. Such objects interrogate the normative placing and ordering of material which binds the social to commodity worship and possession, confounding notions about use and exchange value. Fitting into neither symbolic nor practical orders, these things have escaped the assignations which previously delineated their meaning and purpose and so we are able to relate to them in imaginative, sensual, conjectural and playful fashion – free from the constraining effects of norms surrounding their value or function. We may incorporate them into speculative narratives which free them from epistemological moorings.

The place of objects in ruins thus reveals the extensive ordering of the material world and the ways in which this underpins the social, spatial order discussed in the previous chapter. This is complemented by the preferred ways in which we are supposed to relate to the material world, which largely eclipse a libidinal, sensual, embodied relationship with things in which objects become marked with an excess of meaning and potential usage. As Serematakis declares, a rationalising modernity has perpetrated the 'disordering, institutional repression and perceptual discrediting' of sensual and material experience at a cost to the 'narrative efficacy of material culture' and 'the historical poetics of identity and memory' (Seremetakis, 1994: 136), thereby marginalising and 'discarding (the) sensory values, meaning and emotions attached to discredited materialities' (ibid.). Yet the apprehension of things in ruins decentres the scopic, classificatory modes of sensing which enhance attempts to commodify and regulate the material world, for ruins are replete with multiple affordances which lurk, waiting to break out, bewilder and overwhelm the senses.

The space of the ruin is characterised by multiple relations between things, space, non-human life and humans. The intensities and energies released by these elements impact upon and penetrate each other to produce an ensemble of multiplicities. Accordingly, within this realm, the human body is connected with unfamiliar sensations which disrupt habitual ways of embodiment, establishing temporary connections which defeat a distanced appraisal of the scene. As they circulate and swirl, 'these different types of multiplicities that coexist, interpenetrate and change places' (Deleuze and Guattari, 1987: 36).

–5–

The Spaces of Memory and the Ghosts of Dereliction

I think how little we can hold in mind, how everything is constantly lapsing into oblivion with every extinguished life, how the world is, as it were, draining itself, in that the history of countless places and objects which themselves have no power of memory is never heard, never described or passed on'

Sebald, *Austerlitz*

The Multiple Temporalities of Ruins

In the previous chapters, it has been apparent that ruins, like all places, can be spatially construed in numerous ways and are connected to and connote multiple other places. The temporalities of ruined factories are similarly manifold, for they conjure up various histories, evoke a range of memories, signify obsolescent fashions and products, bear the imprint of the timed schedules of yesteryear, and testify to the natural temporalities imposed by decay and the ecological life cycles of non-human life-forms. Yet ruins do not merely evoke the past. They contain a still and seemingly quiescent present, and they also suggest forebodings, pointing to future erasure and subsequently, the reproduction of space, thus conveying a sense of the transience of all spaces. Current hyperbole insists that the social world is inevitably speeding up, a claim which neglects slower processes, the divergent rhythms which compose the city, some of which are organised to contest the imperative for speed (Highmore, 2002: 175). All activities, people and places are not necessarily caught up by an immersion in flows of velocity. The ruin is not particularly penetrated by the speeded-up mobilities and flows which typify this frantic scenario. Instead, its durability and existence is largely shaped by the rate at which it decays, and it is no longer the site of a production process dominated by future-oriented projects and targets, although these temporal constrictions may be evident enough in the remnants of clocking-in stations, dockets, scheduled programmes of work and delivery, and timetables. Most dramatically, the stillness of

125

ruins provokes a comparison with the fast urban world outside, full of urgent mobilities and social and industrial processes – which require perpetual inputs of energy to keep things efficiently ticking over to ensure profit maximisation. Reversing the temporal order which decrees that which is assigned as waste should be cleared quickly, the ruin produces a slowly accumulating waste. The ruin is a shadow realm of slowness in which things are revealed at a less frantic pace. Within this relative stillness, bypassed by the urban tumult, the intrusions from the past which penetrate the everyday life of the city are able to make themselves felt more keenly.

To explore these overlapping, multiple temporalities, in this chapter I will focus upon the ways in which ruins stimulate multiple memories: recollections which flow into each other and diverge, resonate backwards and forwards, splice the personal and the collective. In ruins, the linearity of narrating the past is upstaged by a host of intersecting temporalities which 'collide and merge' in a landscape of juxtaposed 'asynchronous moments' (Crang and Travlou, 2001: 161), a spatialisation of memory which involves 'crossing, folding, piercing' (ibid.) rather than sequential organisation. Like previous chapters, this is partly designed to interrogate and critique contemporary social and cultural processes – in this case, of social remembering (see Miszal, 2002, for the numerous social dimensions of memory) and the way in which it is materialised and enacted in place and space – and to put forward an alternative politics of remembering which foregrounds the value of the sensual and the contingent, so as to bypass the ways in which memory is increasingly disembedded from place through commodification, legislation and the production of nostalgia. In order to set the stage for a discussion of how the kinds of memories stimulated in ruins might be used to critically assess dominant ways of producing memory in space, I will sketch out some of the contemporary ways in which social memory is externalised through the intensification of commodification and mediatisation; exploring how legislators and experts recontextualise memories pertinent to specific identities and the processes through which the past is simultaneously erased and (re)produced by the heritage industry.

Theorising Memory in Space

In the present era, memory has been described as becoming increasingly externalised, partly because memorable events, places and objects are produced and sold as commodities. The commodification of memory is evident in the intensified mediatisation of popular symbols, sites, myths and icons, whereby the social production of memory becomes externalised, situated and staged outside the local community, and thus 'makes the old (history) into a specific spectacle, as it does with all exoticism and local particularity' (Augé, 1995). The production of these external or 'prosthetic' (Lansberg, 2000) memories include the intensified

mediatisation of memory by films and television programmes, the selling of 'authentic' and nostalgic commodities, the repackaging of 'historic' districts through urban regeneration, the influence of 'expert' readings of place, and extends to the proliferation of museums and tourist and heritage attractions which provide accounts and audio-visual presentations of the 'way things were'. Pierre Nora (1996) argues that these commemorative processes replace memories that are embedded in everyday habits, traditions and social interactions, and are (largely orally) transmitted in place (or *lieux de memoire*). These external prompts to remember are part of the development of a global consumer culture which disembeds social processes from localities and redistributes social remembering across space. Paradoxically, they are also a response to an emergent sense of detachment and displacement which such disembedding tendencies produce, stimulating people to seek to realign places with the past.

An obvious sign of this search for reattachment is what we might call the 'nostalgia industry', comprising a loosely related range of commercial and mediated productions which collectively constitute a kind of communal representational and material resource bank stocked with a host of intertextual elements. It is through the media that a vast intertextuality between the reference points – historic sites, persons, styles, events – is assembled to stretch processes of memory across space.

Whereas the dominant forms of remembering were previously through oral and written modes, it is now the electronic media which frames remembrance, apparently symptomatic of wider processes of disembedding (Giddens, 1991). The commercial search for continuity amongst the threads of discontinuity cannibalises the past for selective material which is used to peddle simulated commodities and media products. Nostalgic themes produced often reinforce certain ideological assumptions about the past, constituting, for instance, idealised narratives and other representations of the rosy and active childhoods of yesteryear, the golden years of empire, previous eras blessed by virtuous moral standards and politeness, a picture-perfect rurality devoid of despoliation, or a time of graceful living and cultivated tastes. These and other romantic notions circulate through many commercial and mediated productions and, to sell things and places, must avoid the suggestion that there were equally negative aspects of the past. These nostalgic images and characteristics percolate numerous popular cultural forms: adverts promoting nuclear 'cereal packet families', soap operas depicting tight-knit communities where activities revolve around pubs and street corners, and 'traditional' styles of home furnishing and gardening. Again, such idealised forms capitalise on widespread fears that the apparent sureties of the past are disappearing, 'diffusing discontent with sentiment' (Tannock, 1995: 459). For instance, strikingly, the nostalgia industry manufactures products that are identified as embodying an 'authenticity' in contradistinction to a present of artifice and fakery, in which the 'real' seems difficult to find or identify. This neurosis that a speeded-up modernity has produced increasing inauthenticity, precisely through the detachment from place and a presumed more stable social reality, means that 'real' ales, bread and holidays possess a comforting appeal, as do notions of 'authentic' places.

As part of the sense that the world is speeding up, the commodification of the past seems to increasingly focus on that which has just passed into history. In this sense, the past has become ever closer as more recent decades are identified and the production of images from recent events are repackaged to become the focus of nostalgic consumption. This can be seen in the search for artefacts from the 1960s to the 1990s. 'Classic' rock music stations and 'gold' television channels, potted programmes about specific decades or years, adverts which 'ironically' comment on older advertising styles, children's toys, sports quizzes and remakes of older movies testify to this cannibalisation of a more recent past. This nostalgia for that which has just happened seems to refer back to what was earlier identified as an accelerated 'archaeology' in which the recent past becomes ancient history in the endless production of the 'new'. And yet, ironically, this nostalgic commodification of a past known and experienced by its consumers as that which is 'old' is simultaneously a 'new' kind of product in its lack of temporal distance from that which it commodifies. These repackagings of the recent seem best captured by Nowotny's (1994) identification of an 'extended present' where the future can never be imagined before it is already upon us. Here the lack of distance between the present and the past produces a temporal context in which we are already nostalgic for yesterday, without any time for critically assessing particular events and trends.

Besides the intensified processes of commodification, the externalisation of memory can also be accounted for by the rise of modern forms of historical expertise which particularly impact upon the ways in which place is remembered. For when 'universal', rigorous, scientific techniques are applied to the classification of objects and places, archives and archaeological traces, they tend to predominate over local memories or even efface them. Whilst these 'legislators' are increasingly being replaced by 'interpreters' (Bauman, 1987), the application of hierarchical forms of knowledge from without removes the sensual, situated transmission through which places, events and people are remembered. These expert accounts replace a remembering which 'takes place in the concrete, in spaces, gestures, images and objects', in the dense socialities of everyday life, for 'history binds itself strictly to temporal continuities, to progressions and relations between things' (Nora, 1989: 9). I have written elsewhere about the 'borestone' at Bannockburn Heritage Centre, allegedly the exact place at which Robert the Bruce

rested his sword before his Scottish army's victory over the English forces in 1314 (Edensor, 1997). Formerly the chief attraction at Bannockburn, this symbolic stone was the subject of scholarly treatises, poems and reveries and was the focus of the site, a commemorative artefact around which individual acts of remembering and collective commemorations took place. Now, however, it is only visible in the form of stone fragments placed in a glass case in the heritage centre. The 'discursive' authority of 'experts' has denied the authenticity of the borestone and thus it can no longer serve as a focal point for remembrance. It has been erased as a mythical symbol by the quest for scientific accuracy and, in Nora's terminology, 'history' has prevailed over 'myth', and the disembedding hand of the external expert has diminished local practice at the site.

A conventional politics of remembering in cities and across space more broadly, has focused upon the construction of specific 'memoryscapes', which materialise memory by assembling iconographic forms and producing stages for organising a relationship with the past. Memorials follow different semiotic conventions and articulate particular meanings which reflect the iconographic conventions of the era in which they were built. Yet public familiarity with the rhetoric of such material statements can decline and they are interpreted according to contemporary understandings (for instance, see Warner, 1993). Nevertheless, the traditions of

memorialisation within the landscape assign specific sites for collective remembering, including war memorials, monuments to the great and the good (often soldiers, statesmen, philanthropists, industrialists and scientists), and statues of military heroes. These spaces typically prioritise particular characters and events as part of a politics of memory drenched in masculinised ideologies and icons (Edensor and Kothari, 1996). These encoded spaces complement the museums, heritage sites and retail spaces, commodified to embody a history of power through which specific memories have been materialised in the urban landscape. And they also consolidate the idea, coterminous with the functional designation of the specific purposes of 'purified' sections of the city, that there are places for remembering and places where memories and the past are irrelevant, places in which redevelopment must be enabled by instant forgetfulness.

This 'traditional' imprinting of memory on space has been expanded latterly by the evolution of a politics of conservation, increasingly allied to the provision of lifestyle regions in cities where status is expressed through the possession and occupation of renovated offices, or formerly industrial or commercial buildings converted into upmarket accommodation. With signatures of the past encoded into lamp-posts, signs and other street furniture, the apparent age-value of location is central to the rehabilitation of such places and the cities in which they occur. The negative inferences of a building characterised as distinctive of an industrial landscape is recontextualised, so as to fit into contemporary designations such as the 'entrepreneurial' or 'post-industrial' city. The fate of many ruins which are not allowed to decay into nothingness or bulldozed into oblivion is to be made over in this fashion. Typically, façades are retained whilst the remainder of the building is gutted, or its skeleton stripped to the bones and reclad with new material. These husks are polished and sandblasted until they blend with the textures of surrounding buildings, losing the patina which testified to previous usage and the effects of aging. The production of reclaimed historical buildings and whole districts in this way wipes out many traces of the past except for a few selective fragments, so that the landscape as palimpsest can be difficult to decode in its regulated appearance. Where signs of the past are evident, it is frequently the case that they are contextualised and identified as 'heritage' within the renovated space.

According to Stallabrass, '(T)here are a shrinking number of everyday spaces which do not construct eternal presents, where memory is not discarded from moment to moment' (1996: 173). Whilst this may be an exaggeration, it nevertheless points to the ways in which specific forms of renovation, customisation, representation and the commodification of historic spaces are enfolded into the spaces of the new as part of a wider politics of memory in which who decides what is remembered and how becomes apparent. For instance these partially, conditionally remembered, recontextualised spaces are remembered *by* developers and experts *for* middle-class inhabitants, businesses associated with places, shoppers and

tourists. This raises wider questions about which spatial and material debris is incinerated, neglected, consigned to dumps or buried, and which fragments are relocated in archives, collections, antique stores, museums, heritage attractions, display cases and lifestyle accoutrements – thereby passing into social and institutional memory. As discussed in the previous chapter, that which has been designated as 'rubbish' is institutionally discarded. As O'Brien claims, '(L)andfills are graveyards for the poor's personal histories and incinerators their crematoria' (1999: 265). The derided popular cultures of yesteryear, the objects that emerge out of working-class cultures and the spaces where they are played out have largely been erased and only recently has there been any tendency to reclaim them – usually in the form of museumised spaces. The spaces of working-class political action have similarly been eradicated from spatial commemoration, the lives of the poor are largely forgotten and those of the wealthy are often celebrated.

Lowenthal declares that historical sites

remain essential bridges between then and now. They confirm or deny what we think of it, symbolise or memorialise communal links over time, and provide archaeological metaphors that illumine the process of history and memory. (1985: xxiii)

How such sites memorialise the past however, what metaphors are used, what is illuminated, and what symbols and myths are available for interpretation are questions that foreground the exercise of power over remembering and forgetting. Who and what is commemorated and forgotten by such inscriptions? Are such iconic forms 'condensation symbols' (Cohen, 1985) which permit flexible interpretation and allow multiple points of identity or are such claims restricted? The manufactured histories that I have outlined above through the imprinting of memory on space through commodification, mediatisation, the construction of 'memoryscapes' and the application of scientific expertise imply a range of imaginary geographies which are largely benign, enduring and uncontested, much like how Lowenthal describes idealised visions of English rurality as insular, enhanced by its long stewardship, stable and ordered (1994). In order to explore some of these questions in more detail, I look at the heritage industry, exemplary in its combination of memorialisation, expert analysis and commodification that I have described above.

As part of the recent massive repackaging of the past through the widespread commodification and mediatisation of images, clothes, artefacts, interior design and food, the heritage industry capitalises on the burgeoning nexus between consumption and leisure in the production of historic places. Furthermore, the saturation of tourist information – comprising guided tours, booklets, interpretative cassettes, information boards, audio-visual presentations, and themed simulacra – attempt to capture the 'feel' of a historical period, evoking events and capturing characters, and thus performing narrative and dramatic fixing. At historic tourist sites, memory is increasingly organised according to 'heritage' which 'fixes' history and potentially limits the interpretative and performative scope of tourists. The temporalities of place are particularly evoked in the foregrounding of the historical, which in certain locations leads to the suggestion that they are 'timeless', a particularly common trope in the marketing of non-Western heritage destinations in travel brochures and advertisements. The identification and establishment of heritage sites thus adds to the contemporary urban topography of remembering.

The heritage industry tends to mobilise specific ways of remembering the pasts of places. In servicing the requirements of commodification and the need to tell a coherent, seamless story about the way things were, heritage banishes ambiguity and the innumerable ways of interpreting the past to compile a series of potted stories and spatially regulated displays. Thus there is an associative imperative to arrest decay, hence to freeze time, best exemplified in the preservation of buildings and forms of urbanity or rurality which are believed to capture a specific and aesthetically championed period. Thus in national parks, heritage districts and at many historic tourist attractions, history is arrested at a particular point so as to evoke a particular theme which excludes what went before and what comes after.

The compilation of that which is worthy of exhibition and valuable tends to involve the collection of only particular fragments, and the subsequent spatialising and ordering of memory by the arrangement of historic pieces in orderly displays, providing accompanying potted accounts, to constitute a sort of official, expert codification which eclipses mystery. This exercise of selecting which fragments are to be exhibited and the very act of re-presentation through placing them in a display case inevitably involves a radical decontextualisation which 'stabilises the identity of a thing' (Thomas, 1991: 4). These exemplary things (exemplary because they are 'best preserved', 'most valuable' or 'most typical') are isolated from their fellow objects as well as taken from the spaces which they inhabit, positioned against uncluttered backgrounds so that they do not co-mingle with other fragments, and highlighted as memorable artefacts for the gaze of onlookers in a 'purportedly neutral space' where they are preserved in an apparently 'permanent state of physical and epistemic status' (Bernier, 2002: 56). And as discussed in the

previous chapter, such an exercise disguises the profusion of excess which objects embody, their excessive material effects and their numerous meanings. Instead, the politics of this sort of exhibition memorialise culture via 'publicly sanctioned narratives' replete with institutionalised rhetoric which masquerades as 'scientific' (Ferguson, 1996).

This spatialising of memory is part of the wider process, discussed in Chapter 3, through which things and space are ordered. The urge to construct purified spaces of this sort stems from modern attempts to accumulate, categorise and exhibit objects and bits of information under one roof, in public sites such as museums. Following ostensibly 'scientific' principles, these modes of ordering different cultures, artefacts and forms of knowledge require the authority of the expert and signify the attempt to banish the randomness of previous forms of display, such as the cabinet of curiosities, which contained heterogeneous objects arranged according to whim. The alliance of scientific method, display and classification, and its transposition into retail technologies and commercial strategies is manifest across urban space, in museums and shop windows alike. The objects in display cases are shiny, separate and alone, masquerading as uniquely desirable and notable, and like commodities, they have been packaged and labelled. The museum cabinet and the shop window bring things to light, cast illumination upon that which perhaps has been previously unrecognised, but its importance has been identified and its (singular) meaning decoded by the expert and curated to highlight these designations. The illuminating searchlight of modern science, in its insistence on rendering history, life and things transparent, whilst no doubt valuable in its contribution to the sum of knowledge, tends to subject all spaces to its pitiless glare, fostering the illusion that all might be revealed everywhere. This monumental banishment of the dark and mysterious within such a modern topography leaves little room for gloom and the disordered yet evocative matter which may lurk there.

Organised remembering like this requires the removal of clutter, and this disguises the profusion of matter and meaning. Again, we must enquire about the selection process, about why certain objects have been discarded, which fragments have been selected for display, which oral testimonies and historical accounts tell the story. It then becomes clear that not all things can be reclaimed for heritage, for inevitably we confront 'complex debris that it is impossible to classify within a pedagogical linearity or to lodge within a referential ideology' (de Certeau and Giard, 1998: 135). The desire to vanquish the indeterminate nature of things is exemplified by Dekkers, who stumbles across a rusting locomotive graveyard in South America, which has been left to decay and is overrun with tropical vegetation. This evocative, luscious scene causes him to draw a contrast with the enthusiasm for the organisation of locomotive conservation in Europe, a pursuit through which 'links with the past have been polished out of existence'. In this instance,

'(N)uts and bolts are collected as if they were evidence for a murder trial and then polished to become pieces de resistance in those mausoleums known as railway museums. There the locomotives stand, as inauthentic as can be, too new to be old, yet too old to be new – sterilized, social misfits' (1997: 28–9).

Like other contemporary aspects of producing memory in place, the heritage industry is partly fuelled by nostalgia forged through the desire to slow down time, the keep hold of that which is subject to endless change, to claim, as Huyssen suggests, 'some anchoring space in a world of puzzling and often threatening heterogeneity, non-synchronicity and information overload' (1995: 7). And yet this seems readily to veer towards a reification of past times and things, a sense that things were always better in the past, a point of view which can be mobilised in the building of conservative and nationalistic political projects and ideologies. Again, the past is being used to serve present ends through the construction of a somewhat fixed narrative which like all such stories eclipses the mystery of the past, so that, for instance, 'the ghost is exorcised under the name of "national heritage". Its strangeness is converted into legitimacy' (de Certeau and Giard, 1998: 134).

In addition to this conjunction between the fixing of the meaning and form of places and the narratives which surround them, the principles of displaying the past and other cultures impacted upon the ways in which exhibitionary spaces were negotiated. Bennett shows how the organisation of spaces of knowledge was devised to attain 'new norms of public conduct' (1995: 24). Performative conventions and normative choreographies were co-ordinated by attendants and spatially guided by the layout of display cases, special rooms, information boards and room plans. This ordered staging materialises a linear narrative in the design of exhibitions so that visitors not only consume the principles of classification, but also actively perform a unidirectional dance along devised routes. In the same way that visitors are expected to comport themselves 'appropriately' around 'memoryscapes', the museum encourages visitors 'to comply with a programme of organised walking' (ibid.:186–7) as part of modern regulatory schemes to organise the behaviour of bodies in public space. For the museum displays objects 'in a certain order and in a certain context, prompting the visitor to go through the rooms in sequence, just as the orator passes in review the "places of memory"' (Damish, 1982: 6). Once again, there are parallels with the regulation of much urban space and the instantiation of performative norms. Coterminous with this project was the regulation of those spaces which seemed to disrupt these new preferred performativities. Spaces of public entertainment, such as fairs and carnivals with their 'heteroclite objects', teeming activities, fleeting and surprising momentary sights and juxtapositions, were 'pruned and replanted at the margins of society' (Shields, 1991: 86). Now, as then, though, the removal of 'gross' and 'vulgar' elements is usually accompanied by a corresponding attraction towards them as objects of 'nostalgia, longing and desire' (Stallybrass and White, 1986: 191); they are sought

out at a variety of sites and spaces, as is evident in the carnivalesque uses made of the marginal spaces of ruins.

My depiction of the mutation of dominant forms of heritage into a hybrid assemblage devised by the expert, the marketer and the showman neglects those multiplicitous expressions of heritage reclaimed by the powerless. The demise of a memory 'rooted in the soil' (Nora, 1996: 11) has been typified as giving rise to a heritage industry which presents a romantic and rather uncritical, conservative notion of the past suited to pleasurable consumption (Hewison, 1987), although as Samuel (1994) points out, these negative depictions malign the numerous 'alternative' forms of heritage which contest, for instance, the uncritical celebration of the stately home as icon of Englishness and those televised romantic costume dramas. Indeed, heritage is a multiple endeavour which crosses from the official to the popular. And there is no doubt that the new museology has made enormous strides to produce critically reflexive and ethical exhibitions which question selection and established forms of knowledge (see Pearce et al, 1996). However, while my critique here largely encompasses those 'official', ideologically laden versions of the past – what we might term 'Heritage' – critiqued by Hewison (1987) and Wright (1985) amongst others, I also include those subaltern attempts to reclaim the past by producing 'alternative', 'dissonant' or 'contested' forms of heritage which centre upon particular identities – for instance, based around ethnicity, class, sexuality and gender. These attempts have quite rightly reinstalled neglected subjects into social memory and contested the class, ethnic and gendered accounts of official and commodified forms of heritage. However, a compartmentalised heritage specific to particular identities tends to reify the past, suggesting that it directly refers 'to entities that existed in the past, compartmentalised and ready to be claimed, rather than being socially and culturally constructed in identity struggles of the present' (Landzelius, 2003: 206). In conspicuously serving contemporary requirements, there is a retrospective identification of lineages of struggle as if they seamlessly blend into present political and cultural realities. Accordingly, these supplementary micro-narratives also deny the multiplicity and mystery of the past, instead offering routes through which we might situate ourselves in relation to an unfolding, linear trajectory, through the disciplined encoding of polysemic fragments within a particularistic heritage to reaffirm essentialised preconceptions of identity. Thus while I am not trying to present heritage as monolithic, it is important to identify the regular forms which it adopts, for much like my argument about the regulation of space which is in itself unproblematic, it is when such social processes become too dominant that they need to be checked, and I contend that a reified heritage of many types is becoming too dominant an influence in decoding and apprehending the past.

In contradistinction to these orthodox codings of the past, and to the imaginary lineages proposed by hegemonic and 'alternative' versions of heritage, a notion of the past which foregrounds ambiguity, polysemy and multiplicity reveals the devisedness, the value-laden assumptions of forms of heritage which masquerade as common sense. Instead, we might 'disrupt the signifying chains of legitimacy built upon the notion of inheriting a heritage' (Landzelius, 2003: 208) and celebrate the obscurity and unknowability of the past through a 'dis(re)membering' which privileges contingent desires and wanton speculation towards objects and places. Refusing the false securities of a stable and linear past, such an approach celebrates heterogeneous sensations and surprising associations, random connections, the ongoing construction of meaning, and also admits into its orbit the mysterious agency of artefacts, spaces and non-humans from the past. Such a rhizomic tactic permits lateral, contingent connections rather than the causal fixing of relationships between events, spaces, objects and people. In those neglected and forgotten places on the margins, it is particularly important to remember otherwise in order to critique monolithic, monologic forms of heritage and to offer an alternative politics of engaging with the past. For however much heritage attractions adopt new audio-visual techniques to tell stories and contextualise artefacts, reframe and select different objects for display, and try to interpret rather than legislate about what is being gazed upon, their narrative impulse can eclipse the past's alterity. Pre-eminently, my critique focuses upon the spatial and material ordering of memory and place. It should be evident that ruins must remain absent from the re-presentation and selling of heritage. In what I have already described in previous chapters, the sensual affordances of matter, the *ad hoc* constellations of things, the obscure functions of machines and artefacts, the mysterious techniques and the spatial disorderings manifest in ruins can reveal the arbitrary schemes of normative practices of assembling and displaying the past. Just as visiting ruins is a kind of anti-tourism, the ruin itself stands as a sort of anti-heritage.

Besides these evident spaces of commemoration, a far more multiple, nebulous and imaginative sense of memory persists in everyday, undervalued, mundane spaces which are not coded in such a way as to espouse stable meanings and encourage regular social practices. Off the main urban thoroughfares and sites of memory that are mapped onto the city, such spaces can critique the established politics which fix memories by spatialising traces of the past and performing discursive closure upon the meanings of sites. In order to evoke the multiple memories which are stimulated by moving through a ruin and to explore some of the ways in which ruins stimulate forms of remembering which articulate this anti-heritage, I will explore the allegorical power of ruins to interrogate memory, look at the stimulation of involuntary memories, and identify the numerous ghosts which inhabit the haunted space of the ruin.

The Allegorical Resonances of Ruins

> … trauma and discontinuity are fundamental for memory and history, ruins have come to be necessary for linking creativity to the experience of loss at the individual and collective level. Ruins operate as powerful metaphors for absence or rejection and hence, as incentives for reflection or restoration
>
> Settis, *Irresistible Decay*

Ruins are already signs which seem to embody historical process and the temporality of existence. These allegorical resonances, embedded in the ruined and the trashed, 'begin at the end of things, overwhelming the "ordinary" flow of time with inescapable memories and desires' (Stewart, 1996: 95). Charged with an evident transience, ruins of all sorts have long symbolised the inevitability of death and decay, the fragility of life and of the material world. At one level, the ruin itself embodies the events which led to its present state, conjures up the processes which led to the demise of the building, its contents and all that occurred within. Ruins are signs of the power of historical processes upon a place and reveal the transitoriness of history itself. The contextual situatedness which shapes the serial telling of changing stories about the past is matched by the ways in which a decaying building reveals certain historical aspects at any one time as layers peel away and things fall out from their hiding places. Yet like 'caves, labyrinths, grottoes and mineshafts' (Miszal, 2002: 3), ruins are also spatial allegorical manifestations of the very process of remembering, of its impossibilities and its multiplicities. For the labyrinthine and denuded structure of ruins symbolise the workings of memory, for moving through them jumbles up 'many different possibilities and experiences' (Pile, 2002: 114).

In her evocative account of the wrecked landscapes of West Virginia, USA, Kathleen Stewart shows how the vestiges of huts, industry, settlements and other obscure signs of the past provoke thoughts on the nature of memory. For memory, rather than a sequence of happenings which blend into each other as part of a seamlessly recollected and narrated story, is composed of fragments. And like ruins, memory is a continually shifting collage of these fragments, some appearing, others disappearing. The consequence of this ongoing fabrication is that memory necessarily resists any totalisation. Thus via the agency of the ruin 'that remembers', 'history and place, culture and nature converge in a tactile image that conveys not a picture-perfect re-enactment of "living pasts" but the allegorical re-presentation of remembered loss itself' (1996: 90). Sensitivity to this effect provides an empathetic resource for those unfamiliar with the place to conjure commemoration of an imagined past. But for previous habitués, the loss of their own participation in the production and reproduction of place stands as a powerful

testament to their shared past in all its ambiguities and complexities, replete with sensations, habits and the awareness of an atmosphere which cannot be narrated. Radiating loss and intransigence in their fragmenting form, ruins appear spell-bound, petrified as signs which can be read for significance: 'through them, a setting speaks to people, haunts the imagination, whispers and audible lamentation, trembles in expectation' (ibid.: 93).

Crucially, the ruin as an allegory of memory is fragmentary, imperfect, partial and thoroughly incomplete. There is no clear sign that the meaning of the past is self-evident and easy to decode if you possess the necessary expertise. There is an excess of meaning in the remains: a plenitude of fragmented stories, elisions, fantasies, inexplicable objects and possible events which present a history that can begin and end anywhere and refuses the master narratives of history, for instance, of the stories which encapsulate places within cycles of boom, bust and decay.

Benjamin (1973) writes about how the city provides the conditions for the interruption of the normative. Urbanites are apt to be shocked by the unexpected contradictions that occur, surprises which disrupt the routinised performances of everyday social life, and this remains the case despite the intensification of spatial regulation which has gathered pace since the earlier modern era in which Benjamin made his observations. The contradictions and ambiguities suggested by these occurrences can be dealt with through the adoption of what Simmel (1995) terms a 'blasé attitude', whereby city dwellers insulate themselves against the sensory onslaught and the incomprehensible experiences they witness in their daily lives. But these surprises can also be regarded as prolegomena for reflection, in that the disclosures which they bring forth can stimulate a practical and critical reflexivity. Here the unusual juxtapositions, archaic artefacts and styles, and the traces of older ways of doing things that remain in ruinous places are akin to the discarded objects Benjamin located in Parisian arcades. As in the arcades, the material culture of the city provides the 'shared collective spaces where consciousness and unconscious, past and present meet' (McCracken, 2002: 150). As I have been arguing, ruins are surrounded by regulated spaces that are contextualised as habitual and fixed, masquerading as single-purpose and hiding their ambiguities. Lying in the interstices of the regulated city, ruinous (dis)orderings of matter and space lie adjacent to these smoother spaces designed to allay fears of chaos and reinforce epistemological and practical spatial normativities. Some of the functions of such spaces might be connected to memory, as in the heritage sites, memoryscapes and renovated industrial districts I have discussed. But the smoothing over of space also involves the erasure or commodification of the past, and fosters the myth that urban development is progressive; and in so doing, there is a forgetting that things might be otherwise, that elements of the past might have conspired to forge an alternative present. Serving as exemplary spaces that connect past and present, ruins contain numerous discarded objects which can be used to enchant alternative, often ineffable understandings of the past, and they also contain evidence of how things might have been and might yet become.

Outside the habits of urban thinking, being and doing, outside of the endless parade of consumer novelties which depends upon forgetting the last new thing, ruins permit allegorical revelations about the past in the present. To return to Benjamin: as I have mentioned earlier, he values the political aesthetics of montage to bring forth revelatory apprehensions about things and their relationships to each other and the wider world, but he concentrates on the deliberate, skilfully wrought collections assembled by artists who aim to provoke specific connections. Despite the lack of any obvious agent in their assembly, collections of disparate objects in ruins can equally stimulate conjectures and prompt the creation of improvisatory narratives. These conjure up overlooked people, places and processes and reveal unheralded connections between past and present and the submerged potential of the past, stimulating awareness of hidden possibilities. For instance, a sense may emerge of how the now defunct enterprise housed in the ruin prefigures future industrial decline, or it might symbolise the ways in which forms of labour solidarity were outmanoeuvred. A revelation about the intense homeliness evolving out of a warm collectivity might arise, and the evidence of an uncanny, habitual expertise in performing skills which are now arcane might serve as an allegory which suggests radical discontinuities between past and present but also highlights the potential for human endeavour applied otherwise. Moreover, the possibilities of design, of alternative and fortuitous aesthetics, of non-commodified things, of forms of solidarity might be suggested. Through such allegorical material, the 'the "naturalness" of "what actually happened"', in official and dominant accounts 'is defamiliarised and rendered available to political critique and practice' (McCracken, 2002: 163).

There is, no doubt, something of the improvisational in these conjectures and revelations by which inanimate objects intrude into the channelled sensibilities of the everyday, providing allegorical possibilities for a reconfigured remembering of the relationship between past and present that moves between the fantastic, the affective and the utopian, resisting authoritative fixings of the way things were. But as allegories of memory itself, ruins ridicule notions that memory is enduring and stable, and they deride the attempts at mnemonic fixing by those who govern commemorations. Compiled out of changing scraps and fragments, and retold differently depending upon audience, mood and occasion, memory is inherently elusive, and has never summoned up a picture-perfect replay of the past.

Ruins and Involuntary Memories

Along with other less regulated places in which signs of the past have either not been obliterated or contained and deliberately contextualised, ruins are spaces in

which involuntary memories may be stimulated. Involuntary memories – in contrast to the conscious use, transmission and representation of the past – are unpredictable and contingent, and given that they are enmeshed in sensation and vague intimations of previous atmospheres, they are slippery to pin down, to describe and represent. They are the 'sleeping images which spring to life unbidden, and serve as ghostly sentinels of our thought' (Samuel, 1994: 27). Because they are not deliberately sought, involuntary memories can come upon us, blasting us back to the past, but not usually in a fashion that is communicable because it is primarily surrounded by recollections of sensual events and situations and thus beyond language. Often rekindled by sounds, 'atmospheres' and particularly smells, these sharp shocks which bring back the past unexpectedly can be extremely powerful. Whereas voluntarily sought and communicated memory is used to represent the past in a conscious operation, these affective, involuntary memories emerge out of the workings of the unconscious (Game, 1991). Benjamin insists that 'only what has not been experienced explicitly and consciously, what has not happened to the subject as an experience, can become a component of mémoire involuntaire' (1997: 114). Those recorded memories, stored and filed away purposively whether as part of an individual or collective form of commemoration do not figure here. It is precisely because they never were subject to deliberate compilation that involuntary memories surge with such vigour, are recognisable but not categoris-able. They do not contain obvious characteristics that can be distinguished, con-sisting primarily of a 'variety of substances and perspectives', as well as lights, colours, vegetation, heat, air, slender explosions of noises … passages, gestures … All these incidents are half-identifiable: they come from codes which are known but their combination is unique' (Bachelard, 1969: 159).

There is something about moving through unfamiliar space in which the urge to perform the procedures of convention are obviated and the affordances beheld seem to offer the conditions for the evocative eruptions of involuntary memory; perhaps this is why de Certeau claims, '(W)hat does travel ultimately produce if it is not, by a sort of reversal, "an exploration of the deserted places of my memory"…' (1984: 107). In previous chapters I have been keen to point out the charged sensuality of ruins, the prevalence of often initially overpowering smells, profuse and intrusive textures, surfaces, peculiar and delicate soundscapes, and perplexing visual objects, juxtapositions and vistas, all at variance to the sensually ordered world outside. It is in the affordances produced in ruins, and in the conse-quent jarring shocks to the desensualised body that a childish sensuality is engaged. For the sensual and often indefinable recollections of childhood, and the furtive memories of stories and fantasies can be involuntarily resurrected in the welter of movement, sights, sounds and smells. Along with all sorts of other inef-fable sensations, those of being dirty, of contorting of the body in accordance with the ramshackle environment, of picking up and playing with an object – sensations delimited by adult custom – can catapult the individual back to childhood.

Bachelard considers the areas within a house that constitute 'felicitous' and 'eulogised' space, namely those protective, inhabited domestic spaces that embody self and value: 'By remembering "houses" and "rooms", we learn to abide within ourselves' (1969, xxxiii). These 'corners of our world' are the fundamental basis of 'home' and a sense of locality. Within the house there are also particular places that have especial symbolic import. Bedrooms, attics and parlours contain smaller spaces where the sensual experience of texture and micro-atmosphere are absorbed in the dens of childhood imagination. Bachelard says of the house that 'each one of its nooks and corners was a resting-place for daydreams' (1969, 15). The power of these reveries is revealed as 'our memories of former dwelling-places are relived as daydreams' and persist during our lifetime (ibid.: 5–6). I con-sider that the 'felicitous' places of the ruin, the attics, cupboards, store-rooms and offices, unpoliced by other adults, carry some of the sensations experienced in these childish lairs.

I suggest that the power of involuntary memories also lies in other experiences beyond childhood, in the rooms we have lived in, places we have been, things we have handled and the faces we have known but appeared to have entirely forgotten. These experiences, constituting a storehouse of mundane and extraordinary events, mix sensations – and hence bodily memories – together with the recall of overlapping geographies with their reference points, routes and networks. For my part, walking around a ruined factory surprisingly conjures up memories of my grandparents and parents, and a host of other relatives, friends and acquaintances who have experienced factory work and told stories about it. Their bodies dwelt in such places and became habituated to them, traversing their spaces, carrying out everyday actions involving objects and machines. Most European and American adults have not yet reached that point at which memories of industrial life and locality, even second-hand, are a distant memory; and those bodies we may still know, partly forged through their enduring encounters with industrial production, can populate these abandoned spaces in our imagination. These half-remembered recollections from our past and its meshing with the history of others linger in a world which will not for many years, if ever, be entirely post-industrial. The sense of inhabiting such industrial spaces may also be complemented by our own work on production lines and offices, work which by virtue of its habitual and repetitive character is not amenable to conscious commemoration. The mechanical reiteration of tasks becomes absorbed into the body as second nature and although not generally consciously recorded, can re-emerge when certain atmospheres, fixtures, textures and procedures provide a surprising nudge, provoking embodied, sensual memories which would have lain dormant without such stimulation. These surprising intrusions from the past are apt to emerge from apparently long-forgotten sensations, for our 'successive living spaces never disappear completely; we leave them without leaving them because they live in turn, invisible and present, in our memories and in our dreams. They journey with us' (de Certeau and Giard, 1998: 148). It is at such moments 'when the mundane elements of our personal histories take on iconic proportion' (Jones, 2001: 380), partly because of the surprise that they have surfaced at all, announcing themselves as important areas of forgotten experience, and partly because they intersect with the memories of others and evoke a disappearing social process. Memory is 'fragmented and dispersed across these unnoticed routines and contingent moments' (Moran, 2004: 61).

The anarchic intrusions of involuntary memory act to destabilise that which has been recorded and classified as significant, and therefore worthy of remembrance. The variegated atmospheres, aggregations, textures, sounds and smells of ruins mean that they are places in which to remember otherwise, realms rich in potential for the evocation of involuntary memories. Along with other places on the margins of regulated space, ruins are 'points of transition, passages from reason to myth, moments of magic that exist at the interstices of modernity' (McCracken, 2002: 151). Another way in which ruins contain magical stimuli to memory is through the spooky absent presence of the past, the ghosts that swarm through spaces of dereliction, producing the not quite comprehensible and confounding the reason of commodified and expert encodings of history.

The Ghosts of Ruins

I have mentioned that the ordered procedures of the factory evaporate when the site becomes dropped from the wider industrial network and is abandoned, but that the recent habitués of the factory, the workers and managers, are likely to have built up an embodied, routinised sequence of enactions that sedimented their sense of being and doing in place. In order to procure efficient production, the factory required the co-ordinated choreography of workers acting out their different roles, a social ordering of bodies that inculcated regular, temporally specific habits of movement to and from and within the industrial space, interaction with materials, social rituals and conformity to institutionalised breaks and procedures. These repetitive performances are what Connerton (1989) refers to as 'incorporating' rituals, impressed upon the body so as to form part of 'social habit memory'. Although he is primarily referring to commemorative rituals organised to imprint memory on bodies, such as national processions and ceremonies of remembrance, workers in a factory are similarly obliged to observe a range of stylised and repetitive actions regulated by calendrical, verbal and gestural codes. The power of this coerced embodied remembering, according to Connerton, is that the inscription of habit-memory upon the participants' bodies provides 'insurance against the

process of cumulative questioning entailed in all discursive practices' (ibid.: 102), in that it appears to follow the natural order of things. Unlike the interpretative scope for innovation in myths and written histories, such rituals lack scope for improvisation but nevertheless are saturated with ideological norms about what is important to remember. Through such practices, largely unavailable to reflexive consideration, identity is mapped onto familiar space, specifying the relationship between the different participants, and between the performers and the site (and the wider network into which it is incorporated).

Thus, for instance, one way of understanding the spatialisation of memory is through the instantiation of a spatial network organised around local landmarks. This is most obvious where related commemorative structures and monuments are collectively assembled to form memoryscapes, constituting 'points of physical and ideological orientation' that together form 'circuits of memory' (Johnson, 1995: 63) which are enacted. However, it equally applies to how a sense of the local is acquired through the ways in which people orient themselves around functional and symbolic spaces that are also embedded with personal and collective memories. Accordingly, the habitual movements of workers follow routes leading from homes – often in nearby housing – through streets, past shops, across parks and into factory gates, and finally to the work station. The reiteration of largely

unreflexive spatial performances such as these, through which a compendium of similar experiences are obtained through time, become sedimented in the body and are thus not readily banished from habit memory when the factory closes down. And that is why it is likely that such embodied memories remain, perhaps echoing through the different routines those ex-workers have fashioned for themselves, or perhaps evident into the coming into consciousness of a past way of life, fuelled by a reflexivity about what previously was a largely habitual and mechanical approach to the daily rituals of work but is now amenable to reverie and contemplation. The topographies of yesteryear thus reassert themselves in memory, the familiar crowd of industrial buildings and the fixtures and local amenities which supported them and their workforce, and in the ghostly traces of past embodied enactions, to produce a sort of phantom network.

Such apprehensions about the histories of places which intertwine individual, communal and spatial identities, may rebuke negative interpretations of ruined space. As Goin and Raymond (2001) point out, reviled landscapes of dereliction and abandonment may not be perceived negatively for inhabitants for whom they are memorable as a sign of once-thriving industry and a vanished way of life. This may be the case when the former place of occupation and familiarity might be reduced to bits and pieces. The testimony of the ruin is also summoned up by van der Hoorn who, in focusing upon the aftermath of the Berlin Wall's demolition, shows that a building may live on even though it may be 'slashed into pieces, recycled, transformed', for 'it can continue to live in fragmented form and act as an intermediary onto which people can project their memories, frustrations or experiences with regard to the object which used to occupy an important place' (2003: 189–90). In this case, van der Hoorn shows how a fragment of the wall is a souvenir that testifies to participation in the destruction of a loathed entity and the witnessing of a momentous event. The previous denizens of ruined factories might equally want to preserve items that can be salvaged from wrecked spaces, as testaments to working there or being local to the place where such activity took place and witnessing its demise. The use of vestiges through which to remember the inhabited and worked-over space of the past might be particularly important, for as cities are reconstituted by mobile capital and consumer-led policies, they tend to create deterritorialised landscapes that often become illegible for their inhabitants (Allon, 2000).

These embodied memories, forged through habituation to the rhythms of industrial discipline and the spatio-temporal imperatives of the working life, are not simply the imposed strictures upon the body by power, for such routines were also sensually inhabited. The chatter of the workplace, the constant whir of machinery, the songs sung together and all the other elements of the habitual soundscape forged a familiar backdrop to daily routine. Similarly, the textures of matter and space, the usual manoeuvres, the entrenched forms of communication, the friendships and the relations grounded in hierarchy, and all the different timings and spacings were part of that everyday that was initially peculiar and became part of that which is apprehended instinctively as familiar. These 'survivals and local differences' were part of the largely invisible everyday underside of a dynamic modernity (Moran 2004: 55), for the everyday is that sphere in which the modern and the residual coexist. The embroiling of daily life with these routines, procedures and embodied habits, the materialities and spatialities and the distinctive enactments which emerged produced the ordinary everyday of factory experiences which also lives on in bodies that remember and are absent presences in the traces of the habitual which remain. These phantom traces of mundane temporality jar with the progressive and dynamic linear modernity with which they seem to contrast, conjuring up both the cycle of the everyday and the traumatic event of closure which ended it.

These routines and embodied pursuits that reside in the memory of ex-workers are, however, not merely recollected by them but are also communicated by the ghostly traces of their residues. I have already mentioned that the peculiar quiescence of the ruined factory causes one to pay attention, and thereby the soundscape is haunted by an absence of noise. But in addition the layout of the ruined factory, at least before it becomes entirely cluttered with falling debris and decaying matter, is principally that which was laid out to facilitate the enaction of industrial routines. Thus as we walk through the abandoned building, our bodies move along the stairways, passages, shop floors, offices, entrances, canteens and rest-rooms, loading bays and car parks, following in the footsteps of the people who made such intense, regular use of this place. Whilst we are free to roam across all space, now it is no longer carved up into different assignations, we pass over the work stations of previous inhabitants, re-enacting that which was accomplished habitually. And as we perform the past by putting our bodies into its flow, by placing ourselves within it 'memory materialises in the body, in movement' and in so doing, 'it

ceases to be pure memory: it is lived in the present' (Game, 1991: 97). The affordances of the building – its gradients, textures, tactilities, expansiveness or pokiness – impact upon our bodies as well, cajoling them into carrying out particular manoeuvres and conveying a sense of what it was like to dwell and work within such a space. The spirits of those previous inhabitants in a sense thus possess us, guiding and accompanying us in our journey through the ruin. To return to the discussion above concerning heritage, it seems obvious that if such places are cleaned up and subject to interpretative encoding then a feel and empathy for the imagined pursuits and everyday sensual experiences of previous habitués would be limited, because such places will have been partially exorcised of the ghosts which contact us. For these are the haunted environs of ruins, the spaces where absent presences make themselves felt through the sense of space which we intuit, which we can empathetically grasp whether from our own previous work experiences, travel encounters, descriptive stories told by friends and relatives, images from television and film, evocative passages from forgotten novels, or simply inexplicable sensations or vague inferences that we might have felt at some other time and place, or through the material impress of space and things.

It is in such instances, in places that initially seem utterly unfamiliar, that sensations of familiarity emerge in the company of strangeness, thus evoking the uncanny. These uncanny recollections from who-knows-where give the lie to notions that memories are in any sense authentic, identifiably 'real', available for instant replay in the mind or recountable as seamless narratives. And they reveal the intertextualities of memory, the numerous fragments that go into the composition and recomposition of that which is remembered and communicated. These instances 'when the over and done with comes alive, when the blind field comes into view, when your own and another's shadow shines brightly' (Gordon, 1996: 197) intimate that memory is haunted by the social, and is never merely formed

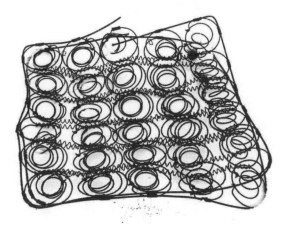

out of the individual recall of essential events, people and places. Such are the 'rememories' that can interrupt a journey even if there is no sense in which they involved you personally. They are the 'profane illuminations' identified by Benjamin (1973). Such uncanny sensations in the face of these ghostly intrusions, both present and absent, also arise because 'we are suddenly faced with no words to articulate the experience' (Buchli and Lucas, 2001: 12).

Whilst ruins can throw up the utterly strange and the very familiar, the uncanniness of that which is frightening and strange but simultaneously comforting and familiar is that which provokes nebulous memories, for to confront such things is to encounter a radical otherness which is also part of ourselves. Partly, this is connected with the alterity of the past and the impossibility of reclaiming it whole, and it is also because traces of our past selves leak out from a present in which we have tried to contain and encode the past. But it is also because ruins are rampantly haunted by a horde of absent presences, a series of signs of the past that cannot be categorised but intuitively grasped, can be read for significance but are ultimately evasive and elusive. These spectres haunt all places. As de Certeau says, there is no place that 'is not haunted by many different spirits, spirits one can "invoke" or not', and he goes further in suggesting that '(H)aunted places are the only ones people can live in' (1984: 108). And as Bell remarks, ghosts are 'a ubiquitous

aspect of the phenomenology of place ... which constitute the specificity of historical sites, of the places where we feel we belong and do not belong, of the boundaries of possession by which we assign ownership and nativeness' (1997: 813). Because of the imperative to bury the past too swiftly in search of the new, modernity is haunted in a particularly urgent fashion by that which has been consigned to irrelevance but demands recognition of its historical impact.

The 'wild objects' which nevertheless continue to populate the city are, according to de Certeau and Giard, 'the equivalent of what the gods of antiquity were, the "spirits" of the place' and '(T)heir silence, their withdrawal from the present, generate narratives about meaning and place' (1998: 135). These things, which have often been taken and uprooted from their original location, inhabit the city, its homes, pubs and gardens, and through this, they transform our 'buildings into haunted houses' (ibid.: 137). Such objects and buildings belong to both present and past, are points of transit between then and now, signifying the multiplicities of the city. But the 'unplanned afterlife of objects' contrasts with the service of objects according to the 'conventional logic of market value, antiquarian interest or personal nostalgia' (Moran, 2004: 62).

In contrast with the ordered city, in the ruin ghosts have not been consigned to the dark corners, attics and drawers, papered over and swept away, reinterpreted and deliberately recontextualised. And because they are no longer inhabited by the human living, ruins are in a state of indeterminacy; the attempted erasure of the past is incomplete and so signs populate these derelict properties. The residues of the accumulated energies expended in manufacture and management are apparent, the signs of toil and the remnant artefacts of production, and this gives rise to a sense that all the invisible energy is stored somewhere awaiting its release, that the impact of the effort and concentration required to make things is trapped in the cold concrete floors or behind the walls.

Ruins are thus spaces in which the visible and the invisible, the material and the immaterial, intersect, for the people who made them, designed them, inhabited them, passed through them, decided to abandon them, and are not there. And yet their absence manifests itself as a presence through the traces, shreds and silent things that remain, in the objects we half recognise or imagine.

As I have already noted, the traces of power are partially etched out on the crumbling structure of the industrial ruin in the banal signs which regulated bodies, in the hierarchies of offices and the divisions between skilled and unskilled work, in the apparatus of routine such as clocking off devices and in machines. Upon seeing these signs of authority, it is easy to conjure up archetypal images of the petty regulators, the foremen and the bosses who have been represented in so many televised and film dramas, as it is to envisage the plump, well-clad denizens of boardrooms, or the recalcitrant workers in an imagined stereotypical drama of factory conflict. This summoning up of a ghostly cast extends to the founders of the factory, the Victorian entrepreneurs who established the enterprise, seeking out backers, and continued to preside over the business. They are joined by their descendants who continued to run the factory, or eventually sold it to larger corporate interests; in either case these parties decided to end production and close down. And the ghosts of utopia reside in the unrealised possibilities that might have emerged from comradely, shared struggle and an elusive wider sense of collectivity, a utopian potential which still lingers in visions of the future. These visions of industrial labour interrupt the glossy images of fashionable, wealthy, middle youth who sit at chic dockside restaurants in the brochures that advertise the charms of the post-industrial, reinvented city whose wine bars, flats and offices

are typically built upon these industrial areas. But they are nevertheless also ghosts that emerge out of the mediations which centre upon space.

Yet whilst there are ghosts who flit through an imagination shaped by popular culture and previous life experiences, there are many other signs of haunting. Some of these are almost imperceptible, such as the skin of workers that remains in the form of dust, the crumbs from their snacks, and miniscule vestiges of blood and sweat produced through work. More powerful haunting presences, however, are the numerous evident traces of the people who formerly inhabited the ruin. The factory tends to be dominated by a functionalist aesthetic, of few frills and decorations, to facilitate the orderly running of daily production, administration, management and timetabling. Thus the remnants of this aesthetic order exist in the styles of office and work station décor, occasionally alleviated by pictures of naked women in masculinised spaces, by schedules or company calendars. The signs of the work carried out in these administrative and manufacturing spaces reside in the silent machines, work benches, palettes, lockers and the apparatus of administration – the filing cabinets, drawers, desks and unplugged telephones.

In another sense of haunting, offices in ruins are often embellished with a outburst of papers, hurled out of their confinement in drawers, a chaotic mess of dockets, order forms, clocking-on cards, prototypes of machines or products, patents, instruction manuals, certificates of inspection, records of wages,

dismissals and disciplinary procedures, advertisements, and a host of other administrative forms. These cascades of displaced paper suggest the activities of a disruptive poltergeist who symbolises the hidden energies of the ruin, whilst also
inadvertently revealing the recent history of a busied administrative staff and its
bosses. Yet occasionally these records linger, damp and mouldering, but largely
untouched, in storerooms, where they have been compiled over many decades. On
such shelves, densely stacked, and in huge ledgers and overstuffed boxes, there are
reams of obsessively stored data, part of the bureaucracy of modern industry.
These ghostly traces of a long industrial history, intimately connected with a local
geography, often detailing the cast of thousands who have successively contributed
to industrial production at the site, are the fading signs of official, administrative
forms of memory, modes of storing information which rely on the systematic
recording of history on paper. This comes as a salutary reminder that the compilation of records via information technology is a recent thing, a somewhat demate-
rialised system of recording which will not be accessible as material vestige
following the demise of any industrial site of production. Equally startling is the
rapid succession of print style and design in these administrative records, even the
type of paper used, into obsolescence. Besides this, however, a confrontation with
this usually banal and repetitive information encoded in shorthand and perfunctory
prose, can be interrupted by records which detail quite jarring historical incidents
which remember people and their situatedness in a past which suddenly seems far
distant. In one such storeroom, in a heavy engineering factory, were the extensive
records of workers and their recruitment and discharge over the second and third
decades of the twentieth century. A Mackenzie left in October 1916 'without
notice because he thought he should have to go before the tribunal for gambling',
in October 1929, J. Malley was hired as a labourer, 'given trial and found unsuitable – too slow', and in March 1928, Dorothy Hadley, aged 14, was sacked
because she was 'warned many times for always wasting time in the yard'. Such
small details provoke whole scenarios populated with a spectral cast.

The functional appearance of the factory cannot belie the fact that this was a
place which people inhabited and domesticated as a kind of homely space. The
ghostly traces of workers' home-making is found in the ways in which space
becomes personalised. At work stations and in communal areas, there are a profusion of attempts at decoration, often flimsy and *ad hoc*, which imprint both individual and collective identity onto space. Lockers and walls are personalised with
stickers, postcards, posters of football teams, newspaper cuttings, photographs of
work events such as parties, cigarette cards, pictures of pop stars and footballers,
betting slips, cards, and nudes, which testifies to a kind of vernacular creativity and
a desire to claim space. There are attempts at art work in crude cartoons of fellow
workers, in collages pasted to the wall, and peremptory sculptures which utilise the
material to hand. These signs of past inhabitation also are communicative: evoke

shared jokes and enthusiasms, and individual eccentricities. Besides these signs, there are forms of graffiti written on the walls which ridicule fellow workmates, sloganise about football teams, imprint nicknames, vilify the bosses and comment ironically on the experience of work. Certain spaces get relabelled as part of this reclaiming: there are Santa's grottoes and goblin's dens. In addition, scribbled onto walls are the working out of sums, lists of products and techniques, which complement the signs identifying which storage areas are designated to contain particular products. The language used in these inscriptions is opaque and mysterious. It testifies to a vanished world in which people knew what these terms and processes meant. The ghostly lore of skilled knowledge, the in-jokes, the banter and favoured slang of workmates are part of what was the unreflexive, sensual, everyday apprehension of factory space, part of the affection between workers, the dense socialities which were reproduced in its inhabitation and are now mute. There are thus a profusion of traces of social interaction and communication which haunt ruined spaces, which are elliptical and peculiar but redolent of the life which seethed there. And as I have mentioned, in ruins these imprints of the personal on space include discarded fashions, crazes, phrases, and trends in popular culture which leap out, unexpectedly rekindling forgotten sensations of handling and

wearing things that have passed into disuse and been consigned to attics, reawakening our own ghostly pasts.

I have mentioned above that there is a sense in which in the present, bodies moving through ruined factories trace out the movements of those who formerly populated such space. Besides these circuits of routine movement which are faintly inscribed in ruins, these bodies are also implied in their traces. The machines and the discarded tools which lie around implicate the embodied skills obtained over time by workers, conjuring up the grasp required to wield heavy implements or the finely-honed skills of intricate work. The intimate relationship between utensil and body, where a kind of hybrid person/tool produces things, is undone by the abandonment of these implements, but bodies and their embedded habits have been fashioned by their interaction with such objects, forging knowing eyes and hands that are at once impossible to apprehend and yet made familiar through an embodied empathy gained by picking up a tool or standing at a machine, and sensing their affordances. These habitual taskscapes, in which close relationships were forged between bodies and tools, are further conjured by the many traces of items of clothing: the overalls, boiler suits, hobnail boots, gloves, hardhats which adorned their working bodies in accordance with the imperatives of production. These absent bodies are further implied by the textures of these remnant articles of clothing – the tears in the fabric of jackets, the patches of grease on the knees of overalls, the muck which cakes corroded gloves, the scuffed exteriors of boots – which again can stimulate an empathetic recouping of the sensory experience of labour in the evident testament to an interaction with industrial space and its properties which remains perceptible. These material accompaniments to their embodied work, everyday presences which were enfolded into bodies in factory life, remain to invoke the ghostly forms of those who wore and wielded them and convey a sensual intimation of the habitus formed through factory work.

Spectral bodies are further summoned by other signs of their impact on space and by fixtures that accommodated them. In the canteens which housed resting bodies, seats and tables remain, bent out of shape through use, as well as the tannin-encrusted mugs workers drank out of and the sinks they used, which remain quiescent since the time of the last supper. Lockers and cloakrooms contain the pegs and hangers which accommodated clothes, packed lunches, newspapers and cigarettes, some of which remain. And the signs of labour can be discerned in the structure of the ruin, in the thumbprints in bricks and the trowel marks in mortar and plaster, the scratches at the work bench and in the repairs made to fixtures. Buttock-shapes remain embedded in more comfortable chairs and the dirt along corridors where legions of workers have rubbed up against the walls bears the traces of passing bodies.

In ruins then, we can identify 'that which appeared to be not there', a host of ghostly signs and traces which let us know that 'a haunting is taking place'

(Gordon, 1997: 8). The ghosts of ruins do not only creep out of attics and shady places unannounced, as is the norm in highly regulated urban spaces, but are abundant in the signs which haunt the present in such a way as to suddenly animate the past. Rather than being exorcised through redevelopment, these ghosts are able to haunt us because they are part of the 'unfinished disposal' (Degen and Hetherington, 2001: 5) of spaces that have been identified as rubbish but not yet cleared. And such things suddenly become animated, when the over and done with comes alive – the things you partly know or have heard about provoke familiar feelings, an imaginative and empathetic recouping of the characters, forms of communication, activities and the sensual experience of factory space. In the haunted peripheries of ruins, these ghosts do not only provoke memories of the epochal and the iconic but recollect the mundane passage of lived factory time in a now derelict space replete with the silence of human inactivity. For instance, as Hal Foster has claimed for the outmoded object which becomes charged with surreal properties and thereby a certain power, it 'might spark a brief profane illumination of a past productive mode, social formation, and structure of feeling – an uncanny return of a historically repressed moment' (Foster, 1993:54)

Conclusion

Telling stories about the past, about people, places and things and sharing them with others is an ontological condition of social life. In order to situate ourselves contingently in relation to place and history, narratives combine collective and individual identities, inserting the personal into the social, and vice versa. Yet the constitution of the narratives through which we make sense of the world is typically structured through different 'time maps' (Zerubavel, 2003) by a repertoire of emplotted stories, which whilst multiple, is nevertheless limited by convention and by what can effectively be communicated. The ways in which incidents and processes are linked to form a story mean that generally, we discern the meaning of any one event only in temporal relationship to other events, creating causal chains of related incidents through which the tale unfolds, rather than the random retelling of disparate kinds of happenstance (Somers, 1994). Some processes of social remembering thus take specific narrative forms, evident, for instance, in the shape given to historical commemorative accounts about nations (from the golden age, to a period of decline, to a coming out of this slough into a brighter future which is informed by the lessons obtained from the golden age), ethnicities and places. Attempts to fix 'official' versions of history pervade popular forms of storytelling in the media and school textbooks. Yet the organisation of remembering, deciding upon which stories are told and how, highlights how such narratives must contingently juggle with historical 'facts' and myths to have any effect, reinforcing established notions of causation. Such narratives are inevitably accompanied by subaltern accounts (by working-class historians, feminists, the colonised, marginalised political factions and other oppressed groups) but they are also subject to contestation, for storytelling is the most *contingent* process of remembering, the most available to improvisation and embellishment. Crucially, the myths which resound through stories tend to be flexible discursive forms, enabling wide scope for interpretation and are ideologically 'chameleon' (Samuel and Thompson, 1990: 3). They may be appropriated to provide antecedence and continuity to widely varying political objectives (Tilly, 1994: 247).

Besides the stories which are orally communicated or written down in authoritative or contesting accounts, memory is also transmitted by its inscription on space through iconic, architectural impression, through the monumental memoryscapes and installations and displays I have discussed. Whilst these commemorative inscriptions are often also surrounded by stories – narrated, for instance, by tour and museum guides – and expert written accounts, passage to and around them is also akin to a narrative, in the sense that de Certeau (1984) infers in his understanding of the ways in which people walk through the city. In this sense, one conception of walking around a ruin might be to construe it as a walk through memory, a walk which also produces a compulsion to attempt to narrate that which is remembered.

Earlier, I quoted Lefebvre's political maxim that 'the most important thing is to multiply the readings of the city' (1996: 159). The raw material of the city, whilst often over-coded and regulated as I have suggested, nevertheless contains multitudinous scraps from which alternative stories might be assembled. That the excess of narrative possibilities is disguised by attempts to fix meaning should not cause us to neglect it. As de Certeau reveals, '(S)tories about places are makeshift things. They are composed with the world's debris'. And even where coded and solidified accounts prevail, they are colonised by 'heterogeneous and even contradictory elements … (T)hings extra and other (details and excesses coming from elsewhere) insert themselves into the accepted framework, the imposed order' (1984: 107). Thus the apparent order of urban space is 'everywhere punched and torn open by ellipses, drifts and leaks of meaning' (ibid.). Such scraps, inconsistencies, eccentricities, incongruities, vestiges contribute to 'the stories and legends that haunt urban space like superfluous or additional inhabitants' (ibid.), and do indeed extend the potential for reading the city otherwise, and open up possibilities for using and representing space in alternative ways.

As imaginary spaces, cities are always informed by fragments of dreams, memories, fears, desires and fantasies:

> the debris of shipwrecked histories still today raise up the ruins of an unknown, strange city. They burst forth within the modernist, massive, homogeneous city like slips of the tongue from an unknown, perhaps unconscious, language' (de Certeau and Giard, 1998, 33).

Whilst it may be difficult to assemble coherent narratives out of these odds and ends, they nevertheless interrupt the stories of historians and other academics, planners, marketers and administrators. To turn such ruined stories into official versions, potted narratives and fixings is almost impossible, for these tales rely upon unforeseen happenings, involuntary memories and revelations, immanent sensations and arbitrary pathways of conjecture and can never pose as authoritative, never aim for closure. And neither can they masquerade as the reflections of a unified subject, since they are more conspicuously invaded by the intersubjectivities of other humans and non-humans. Whilst these incommensurable elements haunt all urban space, it is in ruins that they predominate, thwarting all attempts to construct rigid and coherent stories which fix how a place is remembered. And by looking at ruins we might learn to adopt a more contingent and open approach to reading and narrating urban space, to look for the multiple signs that hide behind the themes and official stories of place. We might also consider the ways in which memory is not merely that which is narrated, that some identities are not necessarily concerned with composing seamless narratives about how they came to be the way they are, and that many dimensions of memory are neither available for inclusion in stories nor even communicable. Memory is thus not always particularly articulate but might be part of broader, less identifiable forms of apprehension, borne out of experiencing structures of feeling grounded in the habitual and the sensual. Stories composed in ruins belong to 'narrativity without linearity, multiple narratives within singular voices and without ultimate agency'. They are

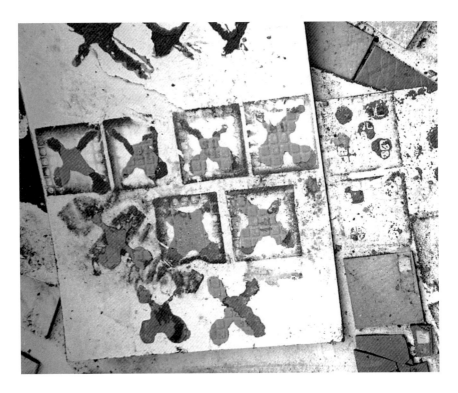

connected to 'spectrality and figuration and (have) little to do with historicism and teleology' (Neville and Villeneuve, 2002: 5–6).

In this regard, ruins foreground the values of inarticulacy. The disparate fragments, juxtapositions, traces, involuntary memories, inferred meanings, uncanny impressions and peculiar atmospheres cannot be woven into a eloquent narrative. Rather like the nature of a ruin, the stories about it must similarly be constituted out of a jumble of disconnected things, occurrences and sensations. Ruins are disarticulated spaces and language can only capture their characteristics through halting speech. Bits of stories suggest themselves and trail away into silence. As an encapsulated narrative, the telling of the ruin's tale from beginning to end is impossible, for such a story must be open-ended. Suggestions about the people, their characteristics and the activities they carried out are multiple yet obscure, but despite this, the enigmatic traces that remain, their ghostly presences, invite us to fill in the blanks. Like the notice boards that under decay suffer from partial erasure but retain certain words, only fragments of stories remain, shaping the kinds of narratives that can be told. And inarticulacy is present in the blurred, partly eradicated legends that advertise products manufactured in the factory, a present indecipherability which mocks the energy expended on fixing meaning through branding and advertising.

This inarticulacy is not an impediment but rather an opportunity to construct narratives out of fragments, to make up stories that seem plausible or fantastic but are not contained by form or convention. More importantly, this vague grasp of what happened and the incomplete tales which are uttered better captures the real impossibility of narrating the past, particularly insofar as this relates to the infinitude of mundane daily experiences. Here the fragments and traces map the erasure of memory, but also evoke 'what in memory is lost when language intervenes – the sensation left by the unfindable' (Klein, 1997: 10), revealing the limitations of narrating memories. For stories in ruins are constructed on the hoof, and so like temporal experience, are not fractured by separate episodes but rather part of a flow of happening, giving the lie to the notion that memory is wholly recoverable, or 'shot through with explanation' (Benjamin, 1973: 89).

The corporate, neo-liberal culture of consumption manufactures identities based on lifestyle, individualism, patriotism, excluded imaginary others, progress and fear of all species of 'otherness'. Yet this is 'continuously interrupted by odd moments of stillness when ears prick up and eyes scan the cultural horizon', for 'strange and inexplicable things are buried beneath the surface of business as usual' – a 'spectral, interstitial residue' which haunts dominant ways of seeing and being (Stewart, 2002: 356). Because it is replete with these interruptions, the kinds of unintelligible signs and improvised stories and memories which emerge from the ruin talk back to other stories about the past. Since the ghosts in ruins bring messages from outside known discourse and its representations (Degen and Hetherington, 2001) they are difficult to weave back into alternative narrative forms. Nevertheless, this very incommensurability means that they are able to decentre commodified, official and sociological descriptions, to conjure up spooky allegories which haunt such narrative fixings, bringing back into consciousness the vague, disjointed stories of the forgotten and the neglected.

Ruins are thus places from which counter-memories can be articulated because, as Gordon says, it is 'essential to see the things and the people who are primarily unseen and banished to the periphery of our social graciousness' (1997: 196). In spatial terms, ruins are consigned to the margins of urban space, and it is there where we must venture if we are to confront the most densely haunted spaces of the city, for 'following the ghosts is about … putting life back in where only a vague memory or a bare trace was visible to those who bothered to look' (ibid.: 22). The people who toiled to manufacture the commodities and the infrastructure of consumer society that is so familiar, are the unheralded, spectral denizens who made the city's wealth. These ghosts, often barely present in the traces they left, stimulate the construction and transmission of stories which are not merely inarticulate but are suffused with affect. For being haunted in this fashion draws us in 'affectively, sometimes against our will and always a bit magically, into the structure of feeling of a reality we come to experience, not as cold knowledge, but as transformative recognition' (ibid.: 8). The knowledge that emerges out of the confrontation with these phantoms is not empiricist, didactic or intellectual but empathetic and sensual, understood at an intuitive and affective level.

The necessity to supplement commodified, official and expert memories and interrogate the principles which underpin their construction, and to imagine beyond these limits backwards and forwards, is not merely accomplished through the fabrication of subaltern accounts which rely on similar principles of 'historical truth' and evidence; it also requires that we 'make things up in the interstices of the factual and the fabulous, the place where the shadow and the act converge' (ibid.: 196–7); in places like ruins. This kind of remembering and storytelling implies an ethics about confronting and understanding otherness which is tactile, imaginative and involuntary. It cannot pretend to be imperialistic because it must be aware of its own contingent sense-making capacities, and because it allows external interruption and sensory invasion, is porous and refuses fixity. Becoming in the ruin involves a politics of producing, representing and imagining space which undertakes a continual enfolding of fragments: bits of ideas, things and sensations that draw up a temporary field of affect that connects with memories and half-understood myths. The objects, spaces and traces found in ruins highlight the radical undecidability of the past, its mystery, but they simultaneously invoke a need to tell stories about it. The difference in the kinds of stories narrated in ruins is that they do not masquerade as seamless or posit sequentiality and causality. Instead, they implicitly acknowledge their own suppositions, fantasies, desires and conjectures. Such reconfigurings of the past may 'implode into the present in ways that unsettle fundamental social imaginary significations' (Landzelius, 2003: 196).

–6–

Conclusion

(The form of ruins) 'must be respected as integrity, embodying a history that must not be denied. In their damaged states they suggest new forms of thought and comprehension, and suggest new conceptions of space that confirm the potential of the human to integrate itself, to be whole and free outside of any predetermined totalising system. There is an ethical and moral commitment in such an existence and therefore a basis for community'

Woods, *War and Architecture*

Throughout this book, I have argued that industrial ruins are an integral part of capitalist expansion, are being produced more rapidly as global production and commodification speeds up, as new products are insistently sought and new markets and more profitable production processes are relentlessly hunted. Whilst they testify to the unevenness of capitalist expansion, revealing sudden local economic recessions within a broader global dynamism which creates grateful recipients of capital flow elsewhere, ruins also signify the sheer waste and inefficiency of using up places, materials and people. Moreover, as glaring signs of instability, ruins deride the pretensions of governments and local authorities to maintain economic prosperity and hence social stability, and give the lie to those myths of endless progress which sustain the heightened form of neo-liberal philosophy through which a globalising capitalist modernity extends. Instead, ruins demonstrate that these processes are inexorably cyclical, whereby the new is rapidly and inevitably transformed into the archaic; what was vibrant is suddenly inert, and all subsides into rubbish in the production of vast quantities of waste.

The ruin marks an end, a sudden fatality, which can be a shock if – like other buildings habitually passed by as part of daily routes – they seem to be enduring fixtures in the landscape. They are thus timely reminders that buildings never last for ever, highlighting the fluidity of the material world. They bring to mind new buildings, constructed to promise future prosperity as they enrol new energies and flows into their orbit, but these too will crumble and decay when they are no longer

deemed economically useful. Perhaps, though, the kinds of new structures that tend to be erected in the contemporary city – the retail sheds and assembly-kit industrial units – will simply be taken apart and reassembled elsewhere, creating an instant gap and erasing any trace of their existence.

To mask this wasting process, the suddenly obsolete, whether space or commodity, is often quickly consigned to history and eradicated from memory, for where this is not the case, the resulting signs of waste – ruins – stand as an alarming rebuke to the visions of progress which insist that all space is ripe for utilisation. Ruins and other forms of 'wasteland' are thus tarnished by their association with economic decline and the failure to quickly replace them with something more contemporary. They cannot be accommodated into the currently preferred flows and planning regimes of the city. Apparently dangerous, ugly and function-less, they are further characterised as spaces for 'deviant' social practices, and as blots on the landscape. Yet I have shown that although they signify the depredations wrought by a destructive capitalism and despite the dystopian prognoses of bureaucrats and planners, there is much of value that can be reclaimed from industrial ruins. For through their very allegorical presence, ruins can cause us to question the normative ways of organising the city and urban life, and they contain within them stimuli for imagining things otherwise. Hidden in ruins are forgotten forms of collectivity and solidarity, lost skills, ways of behaving and feeling, traces of arcane language, and neglected historical and contemporary forms of social enterprise.

Partly this work has been a celebration of ruins as a contribution to studies which foreground a politics of pleasure and sensuality. My interpretation of ruins is informed by different preoccupations to those articulated by earlier celebrants of classical and rural ruins, who mobilised an aesthetic grounded in romanticism and an ethics in which the overwhelming power of God or nature endured, whilst the puny, prideful attempts of humans to achieve immortality disappeared into ruin and oblivion. Although I have taken some critical cues from the gothic perspectives which constitute the most prevalent contemporary appreciation of ruins, I veer away from their dystopian tributes to gloominess and decay: instead concentrating upon the vitality, seething possibilities and manifold forms of life (and past life) which dwell within ruins. And my approach is certainly in opposition to the official, negative designations of ruins as spaces of absence, desuetude and waste.

Ruins stand in rather glaring contrast to the reinvented fabric of much contemporary urban space. For absent in their disordered realms are the usual sheen of aesthetic order, the surveillance of people and non-human life, the placing of things and humans in specific spaces, and the self-conscious awareness that limits

corporeal expression in the midst of others. My contention is not that these processes of ordering and regulating space are unnecessary, or that total disorder should spread across the city. Disordered space can have no value if it is the norm. My point is that these regulatory processes, driven by the extension of commodification, disciplinary cultures, the prevalence of themed and single purpose space, the purification of so many urban spaces, the expulsion of what is superfluous to designed and encoded places, have become too dominant. Urban modernity has been characterised by a tension between the disorder brought by continual change and the flux of urban life with its infinite variety and multiple, incommensurable identities, and the rationalising impulse to classify and rationalise space. In western cities, these latter processes are marginalising the carnivalesque and reducing the degree of interaction with spatial and social diversity. Or else they produce spatial formations in which difference is commodified and contained, and thereby make it difficult to identify the innumerable ambiguities which occur in all social space. Industrial ruins stand as material critiques of these processes, rebuke the shiny images through which the city is marketed, the preferred urban lifestyles and activities. They reveal that the city is not constituted out of an organised web of interconnected, discrete spaces. Instead it includes spaces incommensurable with such containment. For besides ruins, cities also contain scruffy areas behind advertising hoardings, rubbish dumps, undeveloped brownfield sites, culverts and canals, land underneath motorway flyovers, the surroundings of rail lines, junk and scrap yards, and many species of scrubland.

I have attempted to critique these regulatory processes and the urban spaces they produce in three main ways. First of all, I want to contradict common-sense notions that ruins are places of uselessness and emptiness. I have shown how assumptions about the place of plants and animals in the city are interrogated by the rich ecological possibilities of ruins, and the wealth of animal and plant life that can inhabit derelict space. This abundance of nature reveals that the city is never solely a human realm but is criss-crossed by spores, hunting trails and territories, despite eradication programmes. With distinctions between urban and rural consequently becoming blurred, ruins suggest that city space might be produced to accommodate plant and animal life, particularly as the countryside itself becomes increasingly sterile and threatening. In addition, I have discussed how ruins provide unsupervised play spaces for adults and children in which a range of adventurous, carnivalesque activities can be pursued, permitting an engaged sensuous interaction with the materiality of the city and a liberation of the body from urban constraints. Besides these practices, ruins also offer a site for more 'respectable' forms of recreation, including dog-walking and gardening, uses which reveal the dearth of public space in some urban areas, and they can also function as spaces for accommodation and car parking. Furthermore, ruins are utilised for artistic practice, ranging from their casual use by graffiti artists to more

organised schemes which utilise them as temporary galleries. And despite their vilification as spaces of danger, film-makers make wide use of ruins as stage sets for
a range of purposes; through the stories they purvey, images of ruins circulate
through popular culture where they metaphorically articulate particular contemporary themes. Rather than spaces which contain nothing and are useless, it is
apparent that ruins contain a host of unregulated activities which are marginalised
or forbidden elsewhere. They provide an outlet for social practices and forms of
life which are subject to intense scrutiny in other places. Ruins are thus enrolled
into a host of networks which sew them back into the city in new ways.

Secondly, I have shown that in ruins, the normative assignations of people,
things, animals and plants to distinct spaces in which they are supposed to behave
according to prescribed ways, are entirely violated. This shows up the systematic
contextualisation of objects in space, through which they become commodities
and are enrolled into technologies of display. Cities are thus replete with such
orderings, but in ruins, the lack of order can produce insights into how such
regimes operate and foreground alternative ways of placing, suggesting alternative
aesthetics and interactions. In ruins, instead of pre-arranged spectacles, the visual
scene beheld is usually composed of no evident focal point but an array of apparently unrelated things. There are extraordinary and incomprehensible objects
which are not commodities, indecipherable scrawls, obscure functions and sensations to assimilate. This decentring of visual order contrasts with the dominant aesthetic order of the city, for the smooth surfaces and tidy consignment of things to
maintain preferred notions of attractiveness are absent in ruins. Through this aesthetic divergence, the disarray of ruins can promote an awareness of the con-
structedness of normative visual encodings and suggest that there are alternative
ways of looking at space. Other senses are similarly disrupted: the tactilities,
smells and sounds usually experienced are absent and replaced by a sensual order
which initially overwhelms but again acts to critique the expunging of sensual
affordances from the city and foregrounds other, pleasurable ways of sensing the
world. As a further consequence of this sensual disordering, the perfomative conventions of the city must be discarded in the ruin. Given the potential dangers and
the affordances of surfaces, movement can rarely be seamless and out of such dis-
ruptions, and an unreflexive awareness of sensual corporeality may emerge. Such
sensual confrontations point towards an openness towards difference and discom-
fort which engenders a critical perspective towards deeply entrenched bodily enactions and the regulated space which contains them and suggests ways in which the
city might be ordered otherwise. They foster imaginative apprehensions of urban
space, alternative modes of moving through the city and ways of encountering otherness which involve dialogue, creativity and improvisation. Such responses to difference are at variance to the individualistic consumption-oriented practices which
pervade the commodified, regulated, spectacular city

Thirdly, I have looked at how social remembering is inscribed upon the city through the commodification of memory, expertise and mediatisation, processes which act to fix memory and externalise the ways in which people, events, practices and places are remembered. Deeply etched with the power to shape what is forgotten and remembered – a power marked by class, gender and expertise – certain forms of commemoration, notably the increasing production of heritage sites, dominates the imprinting and performance of memory on urban space. I have suggested that industrial ruins are places from which counter-memories can be experienced, although unlike the carefully staged, hegemonic inscriptions of memory upon space, these memories are incommunicable although extremely powerful. Ruins offer different ways of remembering the past. They are already material allegories of the imperfect way in which the past is remembered, replete with loss and confusion. Also, they provoke sensual and involuntary ways of remembering, which gesture towards those impressions and half-remembered bits of knowledge which are just beyond grasp although they may or may not once have been familiar. As such, they cannot be effectively written down and described and therefore contrast with the official and commodified attempts to fix memory, although their propensity to shock us back into a vague past is not inconsiderable. Finally, ruins are inhabited by numerous ghosts, absent presences in the traces of life and work, inarticulate forces which again only offer a hint of the past and

require us to fill in the blanks but give a profound impression of the seething life which surrounded industrial spaces and has largely been forgotten.

In sum, the themes of this book have been organised to offer a broader critique of urban life in a period in which strategies for arranging urban space seem insufficiently nuanced and notions of civic order are gaining a stranglehold which threatens to choke much of the life out of cities. This work is concerned to offer other ways for using and reading the city, for making space in individual ways, creating paths and performing otherwise, sensing, fantasising and desiring in the city, contacting the ghosts and being possessed by them as a means to decentre propriety. Rather than those spaces of ordered disorder, in which the carnivalesque is manufactured and the preferred disposition is a controlled decontrol of the emotions, ruins are spaces in which alternative emotions, senses, socialities, desires, and forms of expressiveness and speculation are provoked by their disorder and affordances.

Putting forward practical suggestions to ameliorate the vilification of ruins and to moderate the excesses of papering over the city and theming space is difficult. The accidental state of ruins is not something that can be legislated for and it seems cranky to argue that decay should be succoured. Nevertheless, the pleasures of ruins indicate that too much urban space is impoverished through prescriptions about which social activities may take place, and it is tainted by the homogeneity of aesthetic encodings which endow space with pre-ordained meaning. Idiosyncrasies and contingencies are an affront to such schemes. The intensity of regulation impedes the occurrence of accidents and things which do not fit in. Ultimately, then, there needs to be a radical overhaul of the urban design process so as to allow difference, oddness and incongruous juxtapositions. A host of alternative forms of public space – in which people may play, mingle, linger and mix with non-humans – are called for, spaces full of objects that are not commodities, spaces whose function is open to interpretation and inarticulate spaces which contain a range of dissident planes, perspectives and textures.

As far as ruins are concerned, there is a case for a politics which allows them to remain, to crumble at their own pace, to ultimately form a gap which reveals where something was in contradistinction to spaces of memorialisation, perhaps somewhat akin to the remnants of spaces retained as wounds which radiate loss in the architecture of Daniel Libeskind (see Merewether, 1997: 37). Such a politics would problematise social memory from the start for it is only through confronting absence, identifying change and acknowledging disappeared potentialities that the rigidities of official forms of commemoration and heritage can be recognised and critiqued. In this fashion, 'the city itself becomes an archival form constituted from the fragments and shards of memory traces' (ibid.) rather than a stage for fixing preferred memories.

Bibliography

Allon, F. (2000), 'Nostalgia unbound: illegibility and the synthetic excess of place', *Continuum: Journal of Media and Cultural Studies*, 14(3): 275–87.

Amato, J. (2000), *Dust: A History of the Small and Invisible*, Berkeley: University of California Press.

Amin, A. and Thrift, N. (2002), *Cities: Reimagining the Urban*, Cambridge: Polity.

Appadurai, A. (ed.), (1986), *The Social Life of Things: Commodities in Cultural Perspective*, Cambridge: Cambridge University Press.

Appadurai, A. (1990), 'Disjuncture and difference in the global cultural economy', in M. Featherstone (ed.),, *Global Culture*, London: Sage.

Assman, A. (2002), 'Beyond the archive', in B. Neville and J. Villeneuve (eds), *Waste-Site Stories: The Recycling of Memory*, Albany: State University of New York Press.

Attfield, J. (2000), *Wild Things: The Material Cultures of Everyday Life*, Oxford: Berg.

Augé, M. (1995), *Non-Places: Introduction to an Anthropology of Supermodernity*, London: Verso.

Bachelard, G. (1969), *The Poetics of Space*, Boston: Beacon Press.

Bataille, G. (1991), *The Accursed Share*, London: Zone Books.

Bauman, Z. (1987), *Legislators and Interpreters*, Cambridge: Polity.

Bauman, Z. (1994), 'Desert spectacular', in Tester, K. (ed.), *The Flâneur*, London: Routledge.

Bell, M. (1997), 'The ghosts of place', *Theory and Society*, 26: 813–36.

Benjamin, W. (1973), *Illuminations*, London: Verso.

Benjamin, W. (1997), *Charles Baudelaire: A Lyric Poet in the Era of High Capitalism*, London: Verso.

Bennett, T. (1995), *The Birth of the Museum*, London: Routledge.

Berman, M. (1982), *All That is Solid Melts into Air*, London: Verso.

Bernier, C. (2002), 'Art and archive: the dissimulation museum', in B. Neville and

J. Villeneuve (eds), *Waste-Site Stories: The Recycling of Memory*, Albany: State University of New York Press.

Bluel, B. (1998), 'St Andrew's Arena', in S. Home (ed.), *Suspect Device: A Reader in Hard Edged Fiction*, London: Serpents Tail.

Boddy, T. (1992), 'Underground and overhead: building the analogous city', in M. Sorkin (ed.), *Variations on a Theme Park*, New York: Hill and Wang.

Bonnett, A. (1989), 'Situationism, geography and poststructuralism', *Environment and Planning D: Society and Space*, 7: 131–46.

Borden, I. (1998), 'Body architecture: skateboarding and the creation of super-architectural space', in J. Hill (ed.), *Occupying Architecture: Between the Architect and the User*, London: Routledge.

Brunsdon, C. (2003), 'Lifestyling Britain: the 8–9 slot on British television', *International Journal of Cultural Studies*, 6(1): 5–23.

Buchli, V. and Lucas, G. (2001), 'The absent present: archaeologies of the contemporary past', in V. Buchli and G. Lucas (eds), *Archaeologies of the Contemporary Past*, London: Routledge.

Buck-Morss, S. (1989), *The Dialectics of Seeing: Walter Benjamin and the Arcades Project*, Cambridge, Mass.: MIT Press.

Casey, E. (2001), 'Between geography and philosophy: What does it mean to be in the place-world', *Annals of the Association of American Geographers*, 9(4): 683–93.

Claessen, C. (1993), *Worlds of Sense: Exploring the Senses in History and Across Cultures*, London: Routledge.

Cloke, P. and Jones, O. (2002), *Tree Cultures*, Oxford: Berg.

Cohen, A. (1985), *The Symbolic Construction of Community*, London: Tavistock.

Connerton, P. (1989), *How Societies Remember*, Cambridge: Cambridge University Press.

Crang. M. and Travlou. P. (2001), 'The city and topologies of memory', *Environment and Planning D: Society and Space*, 19: 161–77.

Cresswell, T. (1996), *In Place / Out of Place: Geography, Ideology and Transgression*, London: University of Minnesota Press.

Cresswell, T. (1997a), 'Weeds, plagues and bodily secretions: A geographical interpretation of metaphors of displacement', *Annals of the Association of American Geographers*, 87(2): 330–45.

Cresswell, T. (1997b), 'Imagining the nomad: mobility and the postmodern primitive', in G. Benko and U. Strohmayer (eds), *Space and Social Theory: Interpreting Modernity and Postmodernity*, Oxford: Blackwell.

Csordas, T. (1994), (ed.), *Embodiment and Experience*, Cambridge: Cambridge University Press.

Damish, H. (1982), 'The museum device: notes on institutional change', *Lotus International*, 35: 6–11.

Dant, T. (1999), *Material Culture in the Social World*, Buckingham: Open University Press.

de Certeau, M. (1984), *The Practice of Everyday Life*, Berkeley: University of California.

de Certeau, M. and Giard, L. (1998), 'Ghosts in the city', in M. de Certeau, L. Giard and P. Mayol, *The Practice of Everyday Life, Volume 2: Living and Cooking*, Minneapolis: Minnesota University Press, pp 133–43

Debord (1987), *Society of the Spectacle*, Exeter: A. Wheaton and Co.

Degen, M. and Hetherington, K. (2001), 'Guest editorial: hauntings', *Space and Culture*, 11/12: 1–6.

Dekkers, M. (1997), *The Way of all Flesh: The Romance of Ruins*, New York: Farrar, Strauss and Giroux.

Deleuze, G. and Guattari, F. (1987), *A Thousand Plateaus: Capitalism and Schizophrenia*, Minneapolis: Minnesota University Press.

Doron, G. (2000), 'The dead zone and the architecture of transgression', *City*, 4(2): 247–63.

Drobnick, J. (2002), 'Toposmia: art, scent and interrogations of spatiality', *Angelaki*, 7(1): 31–46.

Edensor, T. and Kothari, U. (1996), 'The masculinisation of heritage', in V. Kinnaird and D. Hall (eds), *Tourism: A Gender Analysis*, London: Wiley.

Edensor, T. (1997), 'National identity and the politics of memory: remembering Bruce and Wallace in symbolic space', *Environment and Planning D: Society and Space,* 29: 175–94.

Edensor, T. (2005), 'Sensing Tourist Spaces', in C. Minca and T. Oakes (eds), *Tourism and the Paradox of Modernity,* Minneapolis: University of Minnesota Press.

Featherstone, D. (2003), 'Some thoughts on Wandsworth, the land is ours and the inhuman city', http://www.thelandisours.org/campaigns/wandsworth.

Featherstone, M. (1991), *Consumer Culture and Postmodernism*, London: Sage.

Feld, S. (1996), 'Waterfalls of song: an acoustemology of place resounding in Bosavi, Papua New Guinea', in S. Feld and K. Basso (eds), *Senses of Place*, Santa Fe: School of American Research Press.

Felski, R. (2000), 'The Invention of Everyday Life', *New Formations*, 39 (Winter 1999–2000): 15–31.

Ferguson, B. (1996), 'Exhibition rhetorics: material speech and utter sense', in R. Greenberg, B. Ferguson and S. Nairne (eds), *Thinking About Exhibitions*, London: Routledge.

Flusty, S. (1997), 'Building paranoia', in N. Ellin (ed.), *Architecture of Fear*, New York: Princeton Architectural Press.

Foster, H. (1993), *Compulsive Beauty*, Cambridge, MA.: MIT Press.

Foucault, M. (1977), *Discipline and Punish: The Birth of the Prison*, London: Penguin.

Foucault, M. (1986), 'Of other spaces', *Diacritics*, Spring, 16(1): 22–7.

Frykman, J. (1994), 'On the move: the struggle for the body in Sweden', in Seremetakis, C. (ed.), *The Senses Still: Perception and Memory as Material Culture in Modernity*, Chicago: University of Chicago Press.

Frykman, J. and Löfgren, O. (eds) (1996), 'Introduction', in *Forces of Habit: Exploring Everyday Culture*, Lund: Lund University Press.

Fullagar, S. (2001), 'Encountering otherness: embodied affect in Alphonso Lingis' travel writing', *Tourist Studies*, 1(2): 171–83.

Game, A. (1991), *Undoing the Social*, Milton Keynes: Open University Press.

Giddens, A. (1991), *Modernity and Self Identity*, Cambridge: Polity.

Gilbert, O. (1989), *The Ecology of Urban Habitats*, London: Chapman and Hall.

Goin, P. and Raymond, E. (2001), ' Living in anthracite: Mining landscape and a sense of place in Wyoming Valley, Pennsylvania', *The Public Historian*, 23(2): 29–45.

Gordon, A. (1997), *Ghostly Matters*, Minneapolis: University of Minneapolis Press.

Gottdiener, M. (1997), *The Theming of America: Dreams, Visions and Commercial Spaces*, Oxford: Westview Press.

Gregson, N. and Crewe, L. (1997), 'The bargain, the knowledge, and the spectacle: making sense of consumption in the space of the car boot sale', *Environment and Planning D: Society and Space*, 15: 87–112.

Griffiths, H., Poulter, I., and Sibley, D. (2000), 'Feral cats in the city', in C. Philo, C. Wilbert (eds), *Animal Spaces, Beastly Places: New Geographies of Human-animal Relations*, London: Routledge.

Grunenberg, C. (1997), ' Unsolved mysteries: gothic tales from *Frankenstein* to the hair-eating doll', in C. Grunenberg (ed.), *Gothic*, Boston: ICA.

Halfacree, K. (1999), ' "Anarchy doesn't work unless you think about it": intellectual interpretation and DIY culture', *Area*, 31(3): 209–20.

Halgreen, T. (2004), 'Tourists in the concrete desert', in M. Sheller and J. Urry (eds), *Tourism Mobilities: Places to Play, Places in Play*, London: Routledge.

Hannaham, J. (1997), 'Bela Lugosi's dead and I don't feel so good either: Goth and the glorification of suffering in rock music', in C. Grunenberg (ed.), *Gothic*, Boston: ICA.

Harrison, P. (2000), 'Making sense: embodiment and the sensibilities of the everyday', *Environment and Planning D: Society and Space*, 18: 497–517.

Harvey, D. (1989), *The Condition of Postmodernity*, Oxford: Blackwell.

Hauser, S. (2002), 'Waste into heritage', in B. Neville and J. Villeneuve (eds), *Waste-Site Stories: The Recycling of Memory*, Albany: State University of New York Press.

Hawes, L. (1988), 'Intoduction', in *Ruins in British Romantic Art from Wilson to Turner*, Nottingham: Nottingham Castle Museum.

Hawkins, G. and Muecke, S. (2003), 'Introduction: cultural economies of waste', in G. Hawkins and S. Muecke (eds), *Culture and Waste: The Creation and Destruction of Value*, Lanham, Maryland: Rowman and Littlefield.

Hewison, R. (1987), *The Heritage Industry*, London: Methuen.

Highmore, B. (2002), 'Street Life in London: Towards a Rhythmanalysis of London in the Late Nineteenth Century', *New Formations*, 47: 171–93.

Hughes, R. (1980), *The Shock of the New*, London: Thames and Hudson.

Huyssen, A. (1995), *Twilight Memories: Marking Time in a Culture of Amnesia*, London: Routledge.

Ingold, T. and Kurttila, T. (2000), 'Perceiving the environment in Finnish Lapland', *Body and Society*, 3–4: 6.

Jackson, H. (1988), 'Commentary' in *Ruins in British Romantic Art from Wilson to Turner*, Nottingham: Nottingham Castle Museum.

Janowitz, A. (1990), *England's Ruins: Poetic Purpose and the National Landscape*, Oxford: Blackwell.

Jenks, C. and Neves, T. (2000), 'A walk on the wild side: urban ethnography meets the *flâneur*', *Cultural Values*, 4(1): 1–17.

Johnson, N. (1995), 'Cast in stone: monuments, geography and nationalism', *Environment and Planning D: Society and Space*, 13: 51–65.

Jones, J. (2001), 'Consumed with the past: nostalgia, memory and ghostly encounters at the picture palace', *Cultural Studies, Critical Methodologies*, 1(3): 369–91.

Joseph, S. (1988), *Urban Wasteland Now*, London: Civic Trust.

Kabanni, R. (1986), *Europe's Myths of Orient*. London: Pandora.

Kawash, S (1998), 'The homeless body', *Public Culture*, 10(2): 319–39.

Klein, N. (1997), *The History of Forgetting: Los Angeles and the Pleasure of Memory*, London: Verso.

Knabb, K. (ed.), (1981), *Situationist International: Anthology*. California: Bureau of Public Secrets.

Kopytoff, I. (1986), 'The cultural biography of things: commoditization as process', in A. Appadurai (ed.), *The Social Life of Things: Commodities in Cultural Perspective*, Cambridge: Cambridge University Press.

Landzelius, M. (2003), 'Commemorative dis(re)membering: erasing heritage, spatialising disinheritance', *Environment and Planning D: Society and Space*, 21: 195–221.

Lansberg, A. (2001), 'Prosthetic memory: *Total Recall* and *Bladerunner*', in D. Bell and B. Kennedy (eds), *The Cybercultures Reader*, London: Routledge.

Lash, S. (1999), *Another Modernity, A Different Rationality*, Oxford: Blackwell.

Latham, A. (1999), 'The power of distraction: distraction, tactility and habit in the work of Walter Benjamin', *Environment and Planning D: Society and Space*. 17: 451–73.

Latz, A. and Latz, P. (2001), 'Imaginative landscapes out of industrial dereliction', in M. Echenique and A. Saint (eds), *Cities for the New Millennium*, London: Spon Press.

Le Corbusier (1995), 'New York is not a completed city', in Kasinitz, P. (ed.), *Metropolis: Centre and Symbol of Our Times*, Basingstoke: MacMillan.

Lees, L. (1997), 'Ageographia, heterotopia and Vancouver's new public library', *Environment and Planning D: Society and Space*, 15: 321–47.

Lefevbre, H. (1991), *The Production of Space*, Oxford: Blackwell.

Lefebvre, H. (1996), *Writings on Cities*, Oxford: Blackwell.

Lowenthal, D. (1985), *The Past is a Foreign Country*, Cambridge: Cambridge University Press.

Lowenthal, D. (1994), 'European and English landscapes as national symbols', in D. Hooson (ed.), *Geography and National Identity*, Oxford: Blackwell.

Lucas, G. (2002), 'Disposability and dispossession in the Twentieth century', *Journal of Material Culture*, 7(1): 5–22.

MacDonald, A. (1997), 'The new beauty of a sum of possibilities', *Law and Critique*, 8: 141–59.

McCracken, S. (2002), 'The completion of old work: Walter Benjamin and the everyday', *Cultural Critique*, 52, Fall: 145–66.

McGrath, P. (1997), 'Transgression and decay', in C. Grunenberg (ed.), *Gothic*, Boston: ICA.

Maffesoli, M. (1996), *The Time of the Tribes*, London: Sage.

Massey, D. (1993), 'Power-geometry and a progressive sense of place', in J. Bird et al, *Mapping the Futures*, London: Routledge.

Massumi, B. (1996), 'The autonomy of affect', in P. Patton (ed.), *Deleuze: A Critical Reader*, Oxford: Blackwell.

Merewether, C. (1997), 'Traces of Loss', in M. Roth, C. Lyons and C. Merewether, *Irresistible Decay*, Los Angeles: Getty Research Institute.

Miszal, B. (2002), *Theories of Social Remembering*, Maidenhead: Open University Press.

Mitchell D. (1995), 'The end of public space?: People's Park, definitions of the public, and democracy', *Annals of the Association of American Geographers*, 85: 108–33.

Mol, A. and Law, J. (1994), 'Regions, networks and fluids: anaemia and social topology', *Social Studies of Science*, 24: 641–71.

Moran, J. (2004), 'History, memory and the everyday', *Rethinking History*, 8(1): 51–68.

Moser, W. (2002), 'The acculturation of waste', in B. Neville and J. Villeneuve (eds), *Waste-Site Stories: The Recycling of Memory*, Albany: State University of New York Press.

Murdoch, J. (2003), 'Co-constructing the countryside: hybrid networks and the extensive self', in P. Cloke (ed.), *Country Visions*, London: Prentice Hall.

Neilsen, T. (2002), 'The return of the excessive: superfluous landscapes', *Space and Culture*, 5(1): 53–62.

Neville, B. and Villeneuve, J. (2002), 'Introduction: in lieu of waste', in B. Neville and J. Villeneuve (eds), *Waste-Site Stories: The Recycling of Memory*, Albany: State University of New York Press.

Nora, P. (1989), 'Between memory and history: les lieux de memoire', *Representations*, Spring: 7–25.

Nora, P. (1996), 'General introduction: between memory and history', in P. Nora (ed.), *Realms of Memory: Rethinking the French Past, vol 1: Conflicts and Divisions*, New York: Columbia University Press.

Nowotny, H. (1994), *Time: The Modern and Postmodern Experience*, Cambridge: Polity.

O'Brien, M. (1999), 'Rubbish power: towards a sociology of the rubbish society', in J. Hearn and S. Roseneil (eds), *Consuming Cultures: Power and Resistance*, Basingstoke: MacMillan.

Palmer, C. (2003a), 'Placing animals in urban environmental ethics', *Journal of Social Philosophy*, 34(1): 64–78.

Palmer, C. (2003b), 'Colonisation, urbanization and animals', *Philosophy and Geography*, 6(1): 47–58.

Pearce, S. (ed.), (1996), *Interpreting Objects and Collections*, London: Routledge.

Pels, D, Hetherington, K. and Vandenberghe, F. (2002), 'The status of the object: performances, mediations and techniques', *Theory, Culture and Society*,19(5/6): 1–21.

Philo, C. and Wilbert, C. (2000), 'Animal spaces, beastly places: an introduction', in C. Philo and C. Wilbert (eds), *Animal Spaces, Beastly Places: New Geographies of Human-animal Relations*, London: Routledge.

Pile, S. (2002), 'Memory and the city', in J. Campbell and J. Harbord (eds), *Temporalities, Autobiography and Everyday Life*, Manchester: Manchester University Press.

Pinder, D. (2000), '"Old Paris is no more": geographies of spectacle and anti-spectacle', *Antipode*: 357–86.

Ritzer, G. and Liska, A. (1997), '"McDisneyization" and "post-tourism" : complementary perspectives on contempoary tourism', in C. Rojek and J. Urry (eds), *Touring Cultures: Transformations of Travel and Theory*, London: Routledge.

Rojek, C. (1995), *Decentring Leisure*, London: Sage.

Roth, M. (1997), 'Irresistible decay: ruins reclaimed', in M. Roth, C. Lyons and C. Merewether, (eds) *Irresistible Decay*, Los Angeles: Getty Research Institute.

Roth, M., Lyons, C. and Merewether, C. (1997), *Irresistible Decay*, Los Angeles: Getty Research Institute.

Sadler, S. (1998), *The Situationist City*, Cambridge, Massachusetts: MIT Press.

Samuel, R. and Thompson, P. (1990), 'Introduction', in R. Samuel and P. Thompson (eds), *The Myths We Live By*, London: Routledge.

Samuel, R. (1994), *Theatres of Memory*, London: Verso.

Saunders, N. (1995), *Ecstasy and the Dance Culture*, London: Nicholas Saunders.

Seamon, D. (1979), *A Geography of the Lifeworld*, London: Croom Helm.

Sebald, W.G. (2001), *Austerlitz*, London: Penguin.

Sennett, R. (1994), *Flesh and Stone*, London: Faber.

Seremetakis, C. (1994), 'The memory of the senses, part one: marks of the transitory', in C. Seremetakis (ed.), *The Senses Still: Perception and Memory as Material Culture in Modernity*, Chicago: University of Chicago Press.

Settis, S. (1997), 'Foreword', in M. Roth, C. Lyons and C. Merewether, *Irresistible Decay: Ruins Reclaimed*, Los Angeles: Getty Research Institute.

Shields, R. (1991), *Places on the Margin*, London: Routledge.

Sibley, D. (1988), 'Purification of space', *Environment and Planning D: Society and Space*, 6: 409–21.

Simmel, G. (1965), 'The ruin', in K.Wolff (ed.), *Essays on Sociology, Philosophy and Aesthetics*, New York: Harper and Row.

Simmel G (1995), 'The metropolis and mental life', in Kasinitz, P. (ed.), *Metropolis: Centre and Symbol of Our Times*, London: Macmillan.

Somers, M. (1994), 'The narrative constitution of identity: a relational and network approach', *Theory and Society*, 23: 605–49.

Sorkin, M. (1992), 'See you in Disneyland', in M. Sorkin (ed.), *Variations on a Theme Park*, New York: Noonday Press.

Squires, J. (1994), 'Ordering the city', in J.Weeks (ed.), *The Lesser Evil and the Greater Good*, London: Rivers Oram Press.

Stallabrass, J. (1996), *Gargantua: Manufactured Mass Culture*, London: Verso.

Stallybrass, P. and White, A. (1986), *The Politics and Poetics of Transgression*, London: Methuen.

Stanley, C. (1996), 'Spaces and places of the limit: four strategies in the relationship between law and desire', *Economy and Society*, 25(1): 36–63.

Stewart. K. (1996), *A Space on the Side of the Road: Cultural Poetics in an 'Other' America*, Princeton: Princeton University Press.

Stewart, K. (2002), 'Scenes of life/ Kentucky Mountains', *Public Culture*, 14(2): 349–59.

Stewart, S. (1999), 'Prologue: from the museum of touch', in M. Kwint, C. Breward and J. Aynsley (eds), *Material Memories: Designs and Evocation*, Oxford: Berg.

Swyngedouw, E. (2002), 'The strange respectability of the Situationist city in the society of the spectacle', *International Journal of Urban and Regional Research*, 26(1): 153–65

Tagg, J. (1996), 'The city which is not one', in A. King (ed.), *Re-presenting the City: Ethnicity, Capital and Culture in the 21st Century Metropolis*, London: MacMillan.

Tannock, S. (1995), 'Nostalgia critique', *Cultural Studies*, 9(3): 453–64.

Taussig, M. (2003), 'Miasma', in G. Hawkins and S. Muecke (eds), *Culture and Waste: The Creation and Destruction of Value*, Lanham, Maryland: Rowman and Littlefield.

Thomas, N. (1991), *Entangled Objects: Exchange, Material Culture and Colonialism in the Pacific*, Cambridge, PA: Harvard University Press

Thompson, M. (1979), *Rubbish Theory: The Creation and Destruction of Value*, Oxford: Oxford University Press.

Thornton, S. (1995), *Club Cultures: Music, Media and Subcultural Capital*, Cambridge: Polity.

Tilly, C. (1994), 'Afterword: political memories in space and time', in J. Boyarin (ed.), *Remapping Memory: The Politics of Time Space,* Minneapolis: University of Minnesota Press.

Toth, C. (1997), 'Like cancer in the system: industrial gothic, Nine Inch Nails and videotape', in C. Grunenberg (ed.), *Gothic*, Boston: ICA.

Van der Hoorn, M. (2003), 'Exorcizing remains: architectural fragments as intermediaries between history and individual experience', *Journal of Material Culture*, 8(2): 189–231.

Vidal, J. (2003), 'It doesn't look much, but this bleak corner of England is being hailed as England's rainforest', *The Guardian*, 3 May, page 4.

Warner, M. (1993), *Monuments and Maidens*, London: Verso.

Whatmore, S. and Hinchcliffe, S. (2003), 'Living cities: making space for urban nature', *Soundings*, 22: 37–50.

Williams, S. and Bendelow, G. (1998), *The Lived Body: Sociological Themes, Embodied Issues*, London: Routledge.

Wolch, J. (2002), 'Anima Urbis', *Progress in Human Geography*, 26(6): 721–42.

Woods, L. (1990), *War and Architecture*, Princeton: Princeton Architectural Press.

Woodward, C. (2001), *In Ruins*, London: Chatto and Windus.

Wright, P. (1985), *On Living in an Old Country*, London: Verso.

Wylie, J. (2002), 'Becoming icy: Scott and Amundsen's South Polar voyages, 1910–1913', *Cultural Geographies*, 9: 249–65.

Yaeger, P. (2003), 'Trash as archive, trash as enlightenment', in G. Hawkins and S. Muecke (eds), *Culture and Waste: The Creation and Destruction of Value*, Lanham, Maryland: Rowman and Littlefield.

Yudell, R. (1977), 'Body movement', in K. Bloomer and C. Moore (eds), *Body, Memory and Architecture*, London: Yale University Press.

Zerubavel, E. (2003), *Time Maps: Collective Memory and the Social Shape of the Past*, Chicago: University of Chicago Press.

Zucker, P. (1968), *Fascination of Decay: Ruins: Relic-Symbol-Ornament*, Ridgewood, New Jersey: The Gregg Press.

Zukin, S. (1995), *The Culture of Cities,* Oxford: Blackwell.

Websites

British Industrial Ruins
http://www.staffs.ac.uk/schools/humanities_and_soc_sciences/te1
www.wastedspace.org.uk
http:/www.geocities.com/urbexers
http:/www.infiltration.org
http:/www.urbex.org.uk

Index